254

GRACE

GRACE

Robert W. Gleason, S.J.

SHEED AND WARD · NEW YORK

CONTENTS

v

AUTHOR'S FOREWORD

THERE ARE BOOKS on grace which are technical and there are books on grace which are devotional. The present treatment of the subject, although unabashedly technical, has not been aimed at professional theologians, to whose experienced eyes it will offer little that is new or revealing. It is the author's hope, to be sure, that they may read it with indulgence and perhaps even with pleasure, but primarily it is not for them. This book has been written for students of theology, and in particular for the ever growing body of men and women, clerical and lay, who are interested in seeing the profound and abiding questions of theology handled in a more technical way than that to which they have hitherto been accustomed in lectures, articles and books. In a word, this book has been written for seminarians, for graduate students, and for the ever increasing number of educated laity whose intellectual interests are more comprehensive both in depth and in variety. The fact that the many graduate schools of theology now flourishing throughout the country are filled with laymen, priests, religious brothers and sisters is splendid evidence of this new and healthy interest in the theological above the level of the merely devotional and quite definitely on the level of the technical and the scholarly.

Consequently the author can make the assertion that the need for such a work is evident. With a measure of confidence it is his belief that this is the sort of book for which people are eagerly searching. If such indeed proves to be the case, his aim will have been fulfilled.

An additional apologetic note or two should perhaps be given. This book owes a great debt to the best modern and classic works on the subject of grace. To list all would be impossible. To list some few upon which greater reliance has been made, while it may not be of immediate use to the average reader, will at least assure him of the soundness of the works consulted, and may even tempt him to wander on his own in foreign and unlikely-looking fields. Abundant use has been made of the classical articles on grace and justification in the *Dictionnaire de la Bible,* the *Dictionnaire de Théologie Catholique* and the *Dictionnaire Apologétique de la foi catholique.* The sections on the Old Testament owe much to the Old Testament theologies of W. Eichrodt, E. Jacob and Th. C. Vriezen. Many of the historical sections of the book have been greatly helped by Rondet's history of the subject, *Gratia Christi.* The writings of Fr. G. de Broglie and Fr. A. de Bovis on grace have been very helpful with regard to the scholastic theology of grace.

The contents of this book were first drafted as a course of lectures at Fordham University and were then adapted for publication. The subject of grace, so central to Christianity, made appearance in book form all the more desirable since it was felt that the author's approach is in accord with the needs and the taste of the times. In his effort to treat this complex and difficult subject clearly without being too technical, the author has kept the apparatus of scholarship to a minimum. At the close of each chapter he has listed those books and articles which he has found especially helpful. He will be happy if his work will prove useful to the student of theology and the interested layman as an introduction to the beautiful and stirring doctrine at the heart of the Christian mystery—the grace of Christ.

Fratri meo dilecto in Christo Carolo.

GRACE

INTRODUCTION

AT THE TIME St. Thomas was writing there was no clearly organized tract on grace. His own discussions of it occur at the end of his study on ethics, again when he treats of the beatitudes, a third time when he deals with the sacraments, and finally in his treatment of the infused virtues. It was not till the time of the Jansenist heresy and the memorable controversy *De Auxiliis* between Dominican and Jesuit theologians concerning efficacious grace and predestination that the theologians formed the treatise on grace as a result of discussions as to what man could or could not do without it.

Twenty years ago, it was customary to begin with actual grace, the name for the transient helps given by God to preserve us in the state of grace. After these came the study of the state of grace, of the life of grace, and of the various gifts which accompany the life that fills our souls at baptism. Since then, however, there has occurred a refocusing of the entire treatment. The reason for this shift of emphasis is the slackening interest of the twentieth-century mind in the controversies which fascinated the preceding three centuries. The modern theologian chooses to affirm the fact of grace and to study the gifts which accompany it. Nineteenth-century writers sometimes neglected these gifts and, as a result, their treatments of grace tend to be incomplete.

Sanctifying grace is divine life, actual graces are those which assist one in acquiring sanctifying grace, regaining it when lost, and increasing and developing it in its growth towards the beatific vision. Because of its subsidiary role, then, the tract on actual grace should follow that on sanctifying grace. To reverse the procedure is to introduce into the ascetical life, and into the dogmatic, theological life upon which the ascetical life is structured, a misplaced emphasis. Sanctifying grace is radically or virtually heaven itself. It is a patristic adage that grace is the seed of glory, for out of it flowers the beatific vision. It is not merely a pledge of future glory but a foretaste or a kind of a down payment. Actually there is no specific, generic or numerical difference at all between the grace which one possesses on earth and future glory; there is only a difference in state or condition. Grace flowers at death. The wheat is already virtually contained in the seed that is planted; it develops, flowers, flourishes and then brings forth its normal complement. So it is with grace.

Too often in the past the tract on grace has been taught with an almost exclusive Pauline and Augustinian emphasis on its healing qualities, the stress being placed on man's problematic position as a result of original sin. In order to extricate himself from that position and to live a good moral and Christian life, he must receive help from God. For St. Paul and St. Augustine this emphasis was the result of intense personal experience. Both men of forceful temperament, they felt the need for a healing power outside themselves, and they found it only in the grace of Christ. St. John, on the other hand, was a man of a more mystical and placid temperament. He is the prophet of the physical or mystical theory of grace. The focal point in his treatment is not so much the healing qualities as the gifts that accompany sanctifying grace. We are already made sons of God by grace, he says, sons of light, and it has not yet appeared what we shall be. Stressing the idea of grace as an adornment of the soul and as light, he aligns it very closely with charity.

These two aspects of grace are firmly rooted in the Christian tradition; each would be incomplete without the other. But we must maintain the balance between the two. Erring on the side of exaggerated mysticism, we tend to emphasize the gifts that accompany grace, such as the indwelling of the Holy Spirit, the divine friendship, the divine sonship, the participation in the divine nature. As a result not enough attention is given to the need of actual grace and of human coöperation in maintaining and developing the state of grace. Conversely, emphasis on grace as a medicinal force may produce a Christian moralism, an identification of the Christian life with the moral life. Unhappily, much of credal importance then tends to become obscured, with a consequent neglect of dogma and the essentially mystical and supernatural nature of the moral life of the Christian. That life is not an easily discernible and measurable thing. It is simply not possible to sit back and observe the inner attitudes of the soul and there decide with ease our innocence or guilt before God. The Christian life is far more complex than certain Christian moralists have represented it at times.

Specifically, it is not entirely desirable to speak of grace as some "thing" or "that which" goes when mortal sin comes. Sanctifying grace is much more than just a thing; in its essence it is a positive share or participation in the life of God Himself. So there is need for investigating its own nature and dynamics, and for defining it in these terms rather than in terms of sin. Christianity is essentially a positive religion, and all its negations are the shadows of its own light.

All of us are born in a state of loss, of enmity to God—the state of original sin. We do not commit original sin, we contract it; nevertheless it is something intrinsic to us. It is a loss of grace, voluntary not with a personal willfulness but with the willfulness of the choice of Adam. He, as the physical, moral and juridical head of our human family, chose to throw away the family inheritance. As a result, to be born in original sin is to be without the divine life which God has ordained for us. Man's fundamental choice, St. Augustine says, is between himself and God, between contempt of God and contempt of himself. It is conceivable that one's choices in life congeal and crystallize, become the total expression of one's self, in the final choice at the moment of death. Whether or not this is true, whether it is possible or probable, there remains the fact of this single fundamental choice: for oneself or for another, the totally Other, the transcendent God.

It is impossible for man to choose other than himself when he is born in original sin, for this is to exist in a state in which he is turned away from God and therefore deprived of grace. Man comes into existence as a selfish being with a fundamental egotism which he can either exploit and develop or gradually eliminate. He cannot, however, alter the fundamental option by which he is turned in upon himself, unless he receives through baptism that fundamental grace which we call sanctifying. He can, however, perform certain naturally good acts, for some of these (such as loving one's mother) may be easier to perform than to omit.

It is necessary, then, to take a more existential, concrete approach to grace, and it is on the life of grace itself, in its fullness, that this book will center. Preparation for the doctrine was made by God in pre-Christian times, and this development will be sketched. In the course of history the concept of grace has been enriched by Paul, Augustine, Thomas, and others; their views will be integrated with modern theology. The religious upheaval of the Reformation brought much into question, and the Council of Trent labored to clarify and define the traditional doctrine; both subjects are treated in the Appendices, where the tradition of the Eastern Church, as it differs from the development in the West, is also treated. For readers especially interested in the philosophical aspects of grace, an additional note is also appended.

Throughout, the emphasis will be on the double aspect of grace, seen as deriving from the life of God and as a physical reality in the individual soul.

I

THE HISTORICAL
DEVELOPMENT OF GRACE

I

GRACE AND THE
PAGAN

THE CHRISTIAN RELIGION is above all else a dispensation of grace. So central is the concept that almost no aspect of doctrine can be touched upon without mention of grace. Even where the word itself is not used (and Christ Himself did not use it) its thematic importance remains. And wherever the authentic concept of grace has become corrupted, Christianity no longer exists.

Although grace is so specific to Christianity that historians of other religions do not even mention the word, it has nevertheless been foreshadowed in pre-Christian times. This prefiguration is clearly revealed in the Old Testament, and it is perhaps equally evident in the pagan religions of antiquity. The idea of purification, the longing for union with the Godhead, the genuine spirit of prayer, demonstrate man's need for grace and the aptitude of his nature to receive it, if God should graciously bestow it.[1]

A confused aspiration towards grace is present even in those pagan attitudes that are vitiated by superstition, magic and idolatry. In ancient times it was often the task of the philosopher rather than of the priest to maintain the purity of basic religious attitudes. So universal is the tendency of man without revelation to materialize religion and to accent the magical that it is rare to find outside the domain of revelation religious attitudes untainted by pantheism or metaphysical dualism. And although philosophers have frequently cut a path through the jungle of superstition and magic, they have

7

all too often depersonalized religion in the process, making it little more than an ethical culture which reminds man of the contingency of his being—his nothingness—but gives him no inspiration in the search for a personal absolute.

Prayer a Prefiguration of Grace

Yet there are noble expressions of man's dependence on God, of man's sinfulness and need for salvation, in ancient pre-Christian religions. At times such attitudes engender an atmosphere of preparation for the notion of grace. Wherever there is encountered a genuine idea of prayer, we find the liberality and generosity of God appealed to, and the vague realization that humanity has need of divine assistance for the pursuit of a moral life.

Prayer itself, in all peoples, can be seen as a prefiguration of grace. The humble petition for protection and assistance, the simple recognition of sinfulness before God, already prefigure in paganism the answer to its need, which is Christian grace. But where revelation is lacking, man's natural religious tendencies undergo corruption.[2]

The attitude of the Romans to their deities is a striking example. Prayer has become a quasi-automatic ritual, and the gods are assumed to benefit somehow by man's worship and sacrifices. In still other ancient religions man is considered to have been created to preserve the gods in leisure and plenty, to ensure their continued felicity. Such a deformation of authentic religious attitudes witnesses to the tragic situation of man, fallen, needy and ignorant.

But in some of the nobler expressions of ancient religion there is clearly present a mystical élan far superior to egocentric prayer. Despite the self-reliant naturalism evident in much of Buddhism, and its pantheistic overtones, we cannot but be impressed by the profound search for union with God, however falsely conceived, which underlies it. Indeed, its very asceticism is a crude sketch of what Christianity will redirect and purify, just as the mystery of the cross and of identification with Christ will fulfill whatever obscure aspirations to deification underlay it.[3]

Heresies in Antiquity

Almost all the heresies concerned with grace can be seen making their appearance in antiquity, before the concept of grace itself was known. The Roman religion with its accent on self-deliverance and the training of man's liberty, the Stoic indifference and arduous pursuit of self-perfection, already suggest a Pelagius before Pelagius. The risk of deviation is so great that even before the highest representatives of certain schools, a Marcus Aurelius for example, the Christian is ill-at-ease. An Epictetus, for all his noble sentiments, feels no need of prayer. Between the rationalism of the philosopher and the mysticism of the mystery-religions there are many differences of kind, but all are profoundly affected by the absence of the notion of grace. We marvel at the ethical elevation of prayer in Marcus Aurelius, and the obscure search for a personal God, but the same pages that express a consciousness of sin and a longing for goodness offer no answer to the problem of salvation except that of self-effort. Plato, whose philosophic ideas were to serve Christendom well through the medium of the Fathers, had no concept of a beneficent God. Clearly the gods could not love, since love is the child of plenty and of need and the gods have no needs. Nor did Aristotle's impersonal prime mover inspire the Aristotelian to cries of confidence or of piety. Beloved of all, the prime mover loved none, but was rather the initiator of a cosmic, universal movement of attraction. The mysticism of Plato leaves no role for the supernatural, and union with God is envisaged as a natural result of an intellectual *ascesis*. Nothing is found in Plato or Plotinus of the experience of a saving God which God's Chosen People pour forth in the Psalms. There is longing for God, to be sure, and even the sense of sin and of man's lowliness, but not the experience of being loved, cherished, protected.[4]

The philosophies of Plato and Plotinus, and the mystery-religions, undoubtedly sounded in man his need for purification, for union with God, but they were powerless to provide the means. Yet this very powerlessness suggests an obscure appeal for Christian grace. The moral dignity of Stoicism is admirable in itself, but the heavy threat of fate lies over it. The incapacity of nature to fulfill its vocation as a child of God is amply evident in the pre-history of grace. It is Christ who will fulfill; not by destroying, but by purging and leading to their own completion the vague longings implicit in man's relation to God. The universal human longing for union with God will be satisfied not by man's ascent to God but by God's descent to man to incorporate man in Himself.

The Foreseen Merits of Christ

The grace of Christ operated during the period from Adam to Abraham and in pagan times, but in obscure ways. Men were saved by it if they believed, with an assent based on the authority of God, that He rewarded the good and punished the evil. Throughout the centuries of waiting, mankind could always experience the grace of Christ, the Saviour, for God continually engaged in a dialogue with every human heart. Men were judged according to their response to His appeals and solicitations. They either lived in the state of grace derived from the foreseen merits of Christ or they refused the divine invitations and lived in sin.[5]

Divine grace, at this period, was obscurely at work in the context of man's life, reinforcing his natural tendencies to reach out for things of value. The attempts of the pagan to fulfill his own aspirations towards greatness, and other authentic religious impulses, were fostered by the grace of Christ, which led him on to higher aims and a supernatural destiny. Loving and seeking human and personal values, submitting himself to God in adoration, repentance, dependence and gratitude, pagan man was supported by the grace of Christ disguising itself as the greatness of nature seeking its own elevation. In recognizing the providence of God, in confessing a "helping" God, man was already anticipating the figure of the Redeemer. The grace of Christ could marshal all human greatness, all ethical values, and transform them, orientating them to an end above the natural order. Through the natural law, written in the hearts of men, the grace of Christ was secretly and obscurely offered to the Gentile. Many religious, quasi-prophetic voices spoke out in favor of what was most pure in religion and ethics. Sacred symbols and credal content were purified by the interior light that God granted to the pagan, so that he accented what was authentic in religious attitudes and repressed what was erroneous. Nature itself bore testimony to God's existence as the grace of Christ was offered to the pagan silently and in secret.[6]

The time would come when Paul would stand in the middle of the Areopagus, and say:

Men of Athens, I see that in every respect you are extremely religious. For as I was going about and observing objects of your worship, I found also an altar with this inscription: "To the Unknown God." What therefore you worship in ignorance, that I proclaim to you. God, who made the world and all that is in it, since he is Lord of heaven and earth, does not dwell in temples built by hands; neither is he served by human hands as though he were in need of anything, since it is he who gives to all men life and breath and all things. And from one man he has created the whole human race and made them live all over the face of the earth, determining their appointed times and the boundaries of their lands; that they should seek God, and perhaps grope after him and find him, though he is not far from any one of us. For in him we live and move and have our being, as indeed some of your own poets have said, "For we are also his offspring." (Acts 17, verses 22-28.)

But meanwhile the religious situation of man was a wretched one. Polytheism and pantheism, the perversion of sacred rites by magic, immorality and cruelty, threatened his complete ruin. From the moment of the primal catastrophe in Adam God continued to pursue man with His loving intention to recapitulate all things in Christ, to constitute the universe anew with Christ as its center. The mediation of Christ begins, then, with the promise of a redeemer after Adam's fall, and man is saved through faith in the saving and rewarding Christ. His grace is given, even before His coming, by virtue of His high-priestly intercession and His obedience of the cross. But the milieu and circumstances of paganism were unfavorable. Moments of religious grandeur can be found, but there are, on the other hand, pagan prayers demanding of their divinities the satisfaction of man's baser instincts, and frequently they give utterance to a spirit of vengeance and cruelty.

The departmentalization of the gods' functions into carefully specialized tasks, and especially the concept of prayer and worship as a contract between two egotisms, vitiated the ancient approach to God. Some of the Babylonian psalms are of considerable spiritual elevation and many have served as models for the Jewish psalms, but the self-interested, contractual elements in most ancient prayers show how polluted was the atmosphere in paganism which the grace of Christ had to penetrate. Nevertheless the divine gift continued to be offered secretly to the hearts of men, for it was God's eternal purpose that all men be saved and come to the knowledge of the truth. Even in paganism the Church of Christ is, so to speak, prefigured and preformed, however imperfectly and initially, by those who consented to open their hearts to His approaches. Before His coming there are no sacraments of the new law which produce the graces they signify, but man, under the inspiration of the grace of Christ, was free to choose certain sensible signs which prefigured the sacraments, and which designated the subject upon whom God conferred His grace.

Among the intellectuals the persistent temptation was always towards pantheism, as though God shared the nature and fate of the world. Popular religion manifested the downward tendencies of human nature in its fragmentizing of the divine functions, and humanity, in whom the leaven of Christ's grace was at work, was also subject to the solicitations of the Prince of the world, whose aim was to corrupt whatever was valid in pagan religion into idolatry, polytheism, and perversion. If the Brahmins disdained the contractual egotism of many Indians, their own form of self-sufficient pantheism was no closer to authentic spirituality. The risk of deviation, of childishness, was constant.

Throughout this period, as we have said, the grace of Christ proposed for man's acceptance the double certitude that God exists and that He rewards and punishes. In this concept of a saving God is latent the future revelation of the redemptive sacrifice of the cross. The belief in the existence of God contains the secret seed of faith in a triune God whose very life is love. With the grace of Christ inspiring man from within, the marvellous phenomena of nature touched him from without to solicit a response of theological faith in the living God. Paul and Barnabas will remind the Gentiles that His power and divinity are recognizable from the visible world, and that man can then grant God the homage of obedience and faith. But the record of literature shows how often self-interested and anthropomorphic concepts prevailed. Man is seen as the plaything of destiny or the master of his own fate, subject to the jealousy of the gods who cannot endure that his happiness be too great. The shadow of the redeeming cross is over paganism, but it is often obscured by the play of instinctual forces, the egotism and brutality of man. The redemptive grace of Christ works obscurely in the midst of many obstacles.

NOTES

1. H. Rondet, *Gratia Christi* (Paris, Beauchesne, 1948), pp. 23-30.
2. C. Journet, *The Meaning of Grace* (New York, Kenedy, 1960), pp. 81-86.
3. J. Huby, ed., *Christus* (Paris, Beauchesne, 1923); see C. Martindale on Roman Religion, pp. 486-541. Cf. P. Favre in *Histoire des Religions*, ed. M. Brillant and R. Aigrain (Paris, Bloud et Gay, 1953), pp. 410-430.

4. J. Lebreton, "Le monde paien et la conquête chrétienne," *Etudes* (1925), p. 643.

5. P. Arnou, *Le Désir de Dieu dans la Philosophie de Plotin* (Paris, Alcan, 1921), pp. 278-282. Cf. also p. 49.

6. Journet, *op. cit.*, p. 83.

2

GRACE AND THE OLD TESTAMENT

THE CONCEPT OF GRACE has been made to suffer at times from an unreal contrast between the Old and the New Testaments in the light of which the Old Testament is seen as documenting a religion of legalism scarcely even foreshadowing the Christian dispensation of grace. Although this may be true in many respects and in many details, especially of later Judaism, it simply does not apply to the religion of the Old Testament as a whole, and especially to official Jahwism and personal piety.

It is true that it was to take much teaching on the part of Jahweh before His covenanted people would be able to free themselves from materialism in their approach to prayer and sacrifice. The Old Testament prophets bear witness that even the Chosen People tended to feel that the sacrifice of bulls and calves automatically placated God. Yet the superiority of official Jahwism to neighboring religions is constantly manifested in its refusal to mingle magic with ritual. Israel's prayers are free from all constraint of the deity, an element which frequently appeared in the prayers of the peoples who surrounded her.

A Providential Preparation

The entire Old Testament is a progressive, providential preparation for the Christian concept of grace. As the Israelite people became more and more conscious of their sinfulness and their inability to observe the law in its integrity, their prayers anticipate the *infelix ego homo* of St. Paul, revealing the need of a divine remedy which will work in the depths of man's soul to cure his moral impotency:

Within my heart I treasure your promise, that I may not sin against you. Blessed are you, O Lord; teach me your statutes. With my lips I declare all the ordinances of your mouth. In the way of your decrees I rejoice, as much as in all riches. I will meditate on your precepts, and consider your ways. In your statutes I will delight; I will not forget your words.

Be good to your servant, that I may live and keep your words. Open my eyes, that I may consider the wonders of your law. I am a wayfarer of earth; hide not your commands from me. My soul is consumed with longing for your ordinances at all times. You rebuke the accursed proud, who turn away from your commands. Take from me reproach and contempt, for I observe your decrees. Though princes meet and talk against me, your servant meditates on your statutes. Yes, your decrees are my delight; they are my counselors. I lie prostrate in the dust; give me life according to your word. I declared my ways, and you answered me; teach me your statutes. Make me understand the way of your precepts, and I will meditate on your wondrous deeds. My soul weeps for sorrow; strengthen me according to your words. Remove from me the way of falsehood, and favor me with your law. The way of truth I have chosen; I have set your ordinances before me. I cling to your decrees; O Lord, let me not be put to shame. I will run the way of your commands when you give me a docile heart.

Instruct me, O Lord, in the way of your statutes, that I may exactly observe them. Give me discernment, that I may observe your law and keep it with all my heart. Lead me in the path of your commands, for in it I delight. Incline my heart to your decrees and not to gain. Turn away my eyes from seeing what is vain; by your way give me life. Fulfill for your servant your promise to those who fear you. Turn away from me the reproach which I dread, for your ordinances are good. Behold, I long for your precepts; in your justice give me life. (Psalm 118 [119], verses 10-40.)

These lines already show a clear realization that the divine initiative must precede and support human effort and that illumination of heart and intelligence are sought. The more Israel asked of God spiritual blessings rather than worldly goods, the more she became aware of her need for divine assistance to enable her to act faithfully and loyally. From the beginning, conscious that Jahweh summons her to a personal free response of obedience to the covenant, she transcends at once the pagan acceptance of blind necessity. Neither chance nor fate nor brutal necessity governs Israel, but instead a personal God whose dominion extends over the universe and who marshals all creatures, including man's liberty, to serve Him and praise Him. Jahweh is absolute; other gods may be ignored, for they are shadows; vain nothings. In the purity of her mono-Jahwism Israel clears the atmosphere for the appearance of grace.[1]

Because Jahweh is loving, is present, the Israelite may always call upon Him directly and immediately. His providence extends personally to each individual and His justice is unlimited. Even the dim region of Sheol, the after-world, is submissive to His power. Here is the framework for the Christian doctrine of the paternity of God. True, it is the entire people, not the individual, whom Jahweh has adopted, but because of his covenant-relationship to God, each one may call upon Him for fatherly protection. Jahweh has compassion for His people. If a mother can forget the child of her womb, yet Jahweh cannot forget Israel. Even when He punishes empirical Israel, it is to bring about the new Israel, the glorious kingdom of the future. It wounds Him when His spouse Israel is unfaithful, and it grieves Him that He must chastise her. But His love is educative. Despite its infidelities, Israel is His son, His chosen people, sworn to Him as He to Israel. The reproaches He addresses to wayward Israel are the reproaches of one who loves:

Because Israel was a child and I loved him: and I called my son out of Egypt. As they called them, they went away from before their face:

they offered victims to Baalim and sacrificed to idols. And I was like
a foster father to Ephraim, I carried them in my arms: and they knew
not that I healed them. I will draw them with the cords of Adam, with
the bands of love: and I will be to them as one that taketh off the yoke
on their jaws: and I put his meat to him that he might eat. He shall not
return into the land of Egypt, but the Assyrian shall be his king: because
they would not be converted. The sword hath begun in his cities: and
it shall consume his chosen men and shall devour their heads. And my
people shall long for my return: but a yoke shall be put upon them
together, which shall not be taken off. How shall I deal with thee,
O Ephraim? Shall I protect thee, O Israel? How shall I make thee as
Adama? Shall I set thee as Seboim? My heart is turned within me: my
repentance is stirred up. I will not execute the fierceness of my wrath:
I will not return to destroy Ephraim: because I am God and not man:
the holy one in the midst of thee: and I will not enter into the city.
(Osee 11, verses 1-9.)

These tender relations between God and His people stand as a
symbol of those which exist between the Christian and the redeeming
Christ, between the individual soul and the divine action of grace.
The supreme word that sums up the attitude of Jahweh to Israel
is *hesed,* a relationship of fidelity in which Jahweh prefigures the
relationship of Christ to the Christian soul.[2]

The consciousness of sin, the need of repentance, the longing for
God's restoring action, all, by emphasis on the need of a divinizing
and liberating action on God's part, point to grace:

In their affliction they will rise early to me: Come, and let us return
to the Lord: For he hath taken us, and he will heal us: he will strike,
and he will cure us. He will revive us after two days: on the third day
he will raise us up and we shall live in his sight. We shall know and
we shall follow on, that we may know the Lord. His going forth is
prepared as the morning light and he will come to us as the early and
the latter rain to the earth. What shall I do to thee, O Ephraim? What
shall I do to thee, O Juda? Your mercy is as a morning cloud and as

the dew that goeth away in the morning. For this reason have I hewed them by the prophets, I have slain them by the words of my mouth: and thy judgments shall go forth as the light. (Osee 6, verses 1-5.)

The *Miserere* repeats this same sense of total dependence upon Another for salvation and is filled with a humility that we can call Christian in anticipation:

Have mercy on me, O God, in your goodness; in the greatness of your compassion wipe out my offense. Thoroughly wash me from my guilt and of my sin cleanse me. For I acknowledge my offense, and my sin is before me always: "Against you only have I sinned, and done what is evil in your sight"—that you may be justified in your sentence, vindicated when you condemn. (Indeed, in guilt was I born, and in sin my mother conceived me;) behold, you are pleased with sincerity of heart, and in my inmost being you teach me wisdom. Cleanse me of sin with hyssop, that I may be purified; wash me, and I shall be whiter than snow. Let me hear the sounds of joy and gladness; the bones you have crushed shall rejoice. Turn away your face from my sins, and blot out all my guilt. A clean heart create for me, O God, and a steadfast spirit renew within me. Cast me not out from your presence, and your holy spirit take not from me. Give me back the joy of your salvation, and a willing spirit sustain in me. I will teach transgressors your ways, and sinners shall return to you. Free me from blood guilt, O God, my saving God; then my tongue shall revel in your justice. O Lord, open my lips, and my mouth shall proclaim your praise. For you are not pleased with sacrifices; should I offer a holocaust, you would not accept it. My sacrifice, O God, is a contrite spirit; a heart contrite and humbled, O God, you will not spurn. Be bountiful, O Lord, to Sion in your kindness by rebuilding the walls of Jerusalem; then shall you be pleased with due sacrifices, burnt offerings and holocausts; then shall they offer up bullocks on your altar. (Psalm 50 [51].)

In the words of prayers such as this and in the concept of *hesed*, the fidelity of God, we hear and recognize above all the Israelite's deepest yearnings for God's redeeming action, His saving grace.

Concepts of Grace

Although the Old Testament does not have any one word which expresses precisely the reality of grace, and does not define the concept as sharply as does the New Testament, nevertheless the idea of grace is everywhere present in allied concepts. In the Old Testament God's love is envisaged, not as something abstract and conceptual, but as an intensely personal attitude on the part of a supreme being living and present. Jahweh has elected Israel with no thought to her merits and established her in a bond of community-fellowship with Himself.[3]

The words used for this unaccountably free choice of Israel and fidelity to her as Father and Saviour are many. The sovereignly gracious condescension of Jahweh is expressed perhaps best by *hen*, which implies the idea of unmerited favor, supreme generosity. *Hen* cannot be claimed by the suppliant, demanded in justice; the superior, Jahweh, cannot be reproached if He fails to show condescension, for His favor is all generosity. The Old Testament also used the word *ahab* to express the freedom, the self-motivation of Jahweh's love—a word which stresses the element of love whose only motive is love itself. Jahweh chooses to love Israel, and the act of choice is amazing until we reflect that His love is absolutely unconditioned. He loves Israel because He has chosen to love her and has bound Himself to her with an oath. He loves her for His own sake and for His name's sake, perhaps also to set Himself in opposition to lesser gods and to punish the nations. It is *hen* and *ahab* which aptly express the princely love of God for those whose sole claim is their own need.

But the Old Testament comes closest to the full reality of grace in its doctrine of God's fidelity, His *hesed*, His persistent, devoted, loving-kindness to those to whom He has covenanted Himself. *Hesed* is one of the most meaningful words of the Old Testament; it is used of God's dealings with men to sum up the reality in which the covenant is grounded, the foundation without which it could not endure.

The determined, unshakable loyalty of God withstands even the attacks of sinful Israel herself upon the covenant-relationship. Snaith has noted that the single most important and distinctive idea of Israel is God's extraordinary persistence in His faithful love for her in spite of her repeated infidelities. Even if she fails to observe her obligations in this relationship, God holds fast to His loving purpose. By an act of His loving-kindness He has set Himself to judge and to save Israel, to educate her through His self-giving mercy. Because this task is grounded upon the unchanging promise of God, His forgiveness is everlasting, determined, never limited by what is merely legal or equitable. Nor can it be thwarted. Israel is his betrothed, pledged to Him by the law and by His self-bestowal. The persistence of Jahweh's love is founded on the surest of bonds, His eternal promise. Israel is and will be wayward—her infidelity is notorious—but because God's love is unshakable, a new covenant will constantly be given her.[4]

There is no doubt that the reality of *hesed* is closely bound to the idea of the covenant. Although perhaps too much stress has been recently placed on the close connection between the two, and Bultmann's remark that *hesed* is often more nearly the equivalent of grace than of the covenant-promise is closer to the truth, the fact remains that the strong element of fidelity in *hesed* tends normally and naturally to create a bond, a covenant. Certainly this is the conceptual background when it is a question of God's relationship to Israel. His infinite mercy and favor are at the disposal of His faithful love because He has freely elected to establish Israel and Himself in a communion of love.

To Israel *hesed* is no ordinary virtue but has the primacy that charity possesses in the new covenant. Israel's morality is unique, founded as it is on the principle of imitation of the Most High God. For this reason *hesed* becomes the fundamental virtue upon which Israel's national and religious life are based. Embracing every human relationship, it ensures for all a religious foundation. Consequently the upright man is the man who practices *hesed*.[5]

Because of God's irrevocable commitment to Israel the heart of Israelite piety is nothing more nor less than a total response of fidelity. In spite of popular opinion, it is not obedience to the law that is the primary constituent of Israel's religion, but the divine act of self-commitment granting man an approach to God and inviting him to respond with loyalty and faithful love. The law is merely an embodiment, a vehicle, for this faithful commitment on the part of man. The law is grace in the sense that it objectifies Jahweh's free love for Israel and educates man's commitment to Him.

The word, *hesed*, then, which covers so much of the reality of grace in the Old Testament, should not be severed from justice and righteousness. *Sedeqah*, justice, is the expression of man's fidelity to God in an interpersonal framework, for Jahweh is supremely just. The law, which is God's means of bringing Israel to conform to His righteousness, is the concrete pledge of His covenanted fidelity. It is the way to Him, and He will one day write it upon man's heart, so that it will no longer be the divine command which forms the basis of his relations to God, but the new law which He will create by His grace, the inner law of His life, leading men to Him. When Jahweh fulfills His promise in the new covenant men will follow the guidance of His love, given to them in self-donation, and will act almost as if with a second nature, to follow the laws of the covenant. His righteousness and justice are themselves salvific realities, not to be sundered from Jahweh's fidelity. Behind the justice and judgment of God lies the same inexplicable love, accountable only to itself, that we find in *hesed*. Even in later Judaism both justice and fidelity retained their characteristics of a love beyond legal restrictions. The fidelity of man to God could not, even in Judaism, be frozen into a duty-concept of obedience to law. At this period of Judaism, when legalism predominated, the Septuagint usually translated *hesed* as pity or mercy, to retain at least some of the overtones of the Hebrew original.[6]

The close connection between righteousness and fidelity, covenant-love, in Isaias shows how near these terms come to expressing the reality of what the New Testament knows as grace. Because of God's faithful love, his self-commitment to men, man will be righteous. The salvific justice of God will justify the sinner, and the sinner can trust in the loving-kindness of God, while God's fidelity will enable the sinner to respond to God with righteousness. The God of justice is also the *justifying* God, and the sinner may trust Him utterly.

So important is a full understanding of *hesed* that it will be necessary to pursue the concept somewhat further. In its non-religious sense the word refers not to a feeling but to an act: the establishment of a bond implying a mutual commitment. When applied to God *hesed* is usually translated as loving-kindness, to denote a firmly established relationship of love and to emphasize the notion of a perdurable union. Such was the covenant-relationship between God and Israel, wherein the enduring quality is in the constancy of two characters implying a solidarity between them. The typical *hesed*-relationship in the Old Testament exists between God and Abraham. Abraham, man of faith, is one who lives by fidelity to a personal relationship with God observed through a network of obligations. Abraham is faithful in all that God demands of him, even to the sacrifice of Isaac, the child of promise.

On the other hand, in this *hesed*-relationship there is also the loving-kindness, stability and fidelity of God towards Abraham in keeping the covenant to which He has committed Himself. This steadfast, devoted relationship of love between God and man is a theme to which the Old Testament returns again and again. In all its anguish, suffering, exile and grief Israel can take comfort from the knowledge that God is faithful (Osee 2:19-24; 11:1; Jer. 2:2). The most precious thought for Israel in time of desolation is the fidelity of God, the very bond of the covenant. For it is the reality of *hesed* which stands behind the covenant, giving it permanent value and endurance.

What examples of God's fidelity were fixed in Israel's memory? First of all, there was the relationship between God and Adam. In reaching out to Adam after his sin, God shows that His love and mercy remain faithful in spite of Adam's infidelity. Again, when God repents of having made the world and sends the flood, He is still faithful. He does not destroy the inhabitants of the ark but brings them forth and begins again His work of leading all mankind to salvation. The very call of Abraham is that all nations may be blessed in him. For the nations, too, will experience the *hesed* of God.

The legends of Jonas and Ruth attest to the fact that God's loving-kindness is exercised toward Gentile as well as toward Jew. Amos shows that God cares even for the Philistines (Amos 9:7). Deutero-Isaias indicates that God's fidelity embraces all nations. As the history of Israel progresses, revelation widens in time to reveal the promise to Abraham orientated toward the future establishment of the triumphant kingdom of God. Revelation also widens spatially to show that God's *hesed* includes all the nations and even the entire cosmos, for He pours out His mercy and loving-kindness upon all nature: "The earth is full of the mercy of God" (ps. 32 [33]: 5; cf. ps. 135 [136]).

Even the animals will experience God's fidelity: "The wolf shall dwell with the lamb, and the leopard shall lie down with the kid. The calf and the lion and the sheep shall abide together" (Isa. 11: 6). The whole world will ultimately be revivified and glorified by the living God. He will summon the universe to a fullness of splendor, now but potential, to be realized in the establishment of the final kingdom to come.

The English scholar Torrance has called *hesed* the great sacramental word of Old Testament faith because of its intimate connection with the covenant and with the fidelity of God to the individual as well. To the Israelite God was not only an active power but a living person, stable and steadfast. Some authors stress the notion of strength in the concept of God's fidelity, but this must not be considered apart from the idea of merciful, loving kindness. God is seen in the covenant as showing *hesed* (Exod. 34:6-10). Having involved Himself with man, He has committed Himself by the covenant to be faithful to His promises.

Various images are borrowed from human society to represent God's fidelity in the Old Testament. Sometimes it is that of a father towards a son: "When Israel was a child, then I loved him, and called my son out of Egypt" (Osee 11:1). Sometimes the image is that of a mother (Isa. 49:15). Occasionally it is that of a shepherd: "I will seek that which was lost, and that which was driven away, I will bring again. And I will bind up that which was broken, and I will strengthen that which was weak" (Ezech. 34:16). The most frequent image is that of the marital union exemplified by the steadfast, faithful love of Osee for his unfaithful wife: "And I will espouse thee to me forever" (Osee 2:19ff.).

For the Israelite God's *hesed* was so marvellous that the psalmist sang of it as a miracle: "Jahweh has made marvellous his *hesed*" (p.s. 4:4). "Make marvellous thy *hesed*" (ps. 16 [17]:7). "Blessed be Jahweh, for he has made his *hesed* wonderful for me" (ps. 31 [32]:22). The divine fidelity is above all else a persevering love which never weakens and is never taken back. The whole history of Israel is one extraordinary demonstration of this divine fidelity.

Personal Piety

In addition to the sense of sin, the longing for God's liberating action, and the vital concept of His faithfulness to her as a people, strong prefiguration of grace is to be seen in the element of personal piety continually present in Israel. However difficult a task it is to analyze the personal response of man to God in any religion, and particularly in one so remote from us in cultural forms and in national traits, we can nevertheless affirm with certainty that religion in Israel was always a personal affair. They are in error who claim that all of Israel's religion is purely cultic and that the individual plays no role until the very late discovery of the fact by Ezechiel. Beginning with Abraham and Moses, biblical man reveals that his heart is open to God, the details of his daily life referred to Him. From the start, permanent spiritual orientations of the classical mould are visible in Israelite thought and prayer.

Israelite religion is characterized particularly by the spirit of faith; the Israelite is aware that he stands before God; that the Lord whom he serves is a living God. It is also characterized by the virtue of confidence in God. Hebrew man does not feel himself to be a prey to blind, demoniac forces in the world, for he realizes that there is One above him who is supreme and transcendent and whose omnipotence overshadows every detail of personal life. This is true also in the Israelite concept of history; it is not blind fate or destiny which presides over the world but a loving Father whose Providence stretches from end to end mightily. To the Israelite history is not a blind, cyclic repetition, as it was to the Greeks, but a process orientated towards an end, the Messias and the kingdom of Jahweh; hence he plays his role in history accordingly, looking upon all human history as a dialogue with God.

Israelite religion is characterized as well by a sense of humble submission to God. Israelite man realizes that he is nothing before God; a blade of grass which is here today and gone tomorrow, a leaf in the wind; he is resigned to accept from God's hand whatever He sends to him. Job is the classic figure of this resignation. Confronted with the inconclusive arguments of the theologians, his sorrow remains real, undeserved though it is. Yet he never loses sight of the Providence of God.[7]

It is also a mark of Israelite religion to be strongly individualistic and at the same time full of awareness that all are brothers, men of the covenant. Old Testament man must constantly be brought to humility by the prophets, because God's choice of Israel carried with it the ever-present danger of self-enclosure, rigid exclusivism and pride. It is because of God's choice of Israel, His wholly unaccountable love for her, that we can have those prayers, seemingly so strange, in which the Israelite complains to God, holding up his own justice before Him. He does this because he believes that God is a just God Himself; since He is justice personified, He will glorify His own justice by rewarding that of the Israelite.

Joy

Old Testament man is aware of the many frustrations inherent in human life, even to the point of tragedy, but he does not despair. It can even be said that one of the foremost characteristics of Israel's religion is joy. It is exuberant, jubilantly joyous, because Israel feels herself constantly in the presence of the living God, who defines Himself as the One who is here, the One who is present, the One who is with us. In the words of the psalmist: "He who has made the ear, shall He not hear?" In the hymns of Israel and in her rituals, there is an infinitely more varied and exuberant approach to religion than in those of the Greeks. Hymns are accompanied not only by lyres, by fifes and other wind instruments, but also by drums and percussion instruments, and there is singing and even dancing. David himself dances.[8]

Only later does the note of exclusive rigidity come into Israel's religion, when she begins to consider herself a bonded people, and all others destined for damnation. As we have said, the legalistic, narrow approach is really not characteristic of Old Testament religion but of Judaism—that is, the later development, just before and during the time of Our Lord. The Pharisees prepared for prayer by a thousand ritualistic details which had to be followed;

originally, however, Israel would break into spontaneous prayer for any reason—a military victory, for instance, as in the Song of Deborah, or a wedding feast, or a love-song. In their war-songs, their love-songs, their work-songs, God was always present and praised. Later religion came to be confined to the narrow boundaries of a systematized order, but this was the invention of the Pharisees.

Confidence

The first characteristic of Israel's religion was confidence in God. There was a sense of nearness to God; that He could be met easily. Thus Israel loved to pray in sanctuaries, she longed to make the pilgrimage to Jerusalem, where within the temple she faced the Holy of Holies. She had hymns, the very beautiful gradual hymns sung as she approached Jerusalem. But she could meet God anywhere—in natural phenomena, in the wind and the trees and the high places, which called to mind the closeness of heaven. One should read the Psalms to find how clearly this characteristic note of Israel's confidence in God is echoed in her prayer.

Again, Israel's religion is one in which the individual man finds it easy to approach his God personally, as we see from the fact that he addresses Him directly as God, Jahweh, Adonai, Lord, my Lord. This is quite unlike the neighboring religions of the Near East, which were burdened with elaborate court ceremonial before one could even approach to speak to God in prayer, like the long addresses that are still in use in diplomatic circles before one can get to the business at hand. There is also evidence of a personal relationship in the freedom and spontaneity with which persons speak to God. The fact that Job and Jeremias can complain shows that they feel they are spiritually free in their relationships with God. Although they are submissive they have no hesitation, even as Christian saints have none later, in making their complaints heard before the Lord, and then in peace accepting His reply.

There is an admirable freedom of the body for Israel's prayer. She may pray standing, to indicate alertness and readiness to do the will of Jahweh; she may prostrate herself, as a sign of her own nothingness before God: she may lift up her hands in the humble admission that she receives all blessings from the Lord. There is no posture—and even more, there is no occupation—in which she is not at liberty to pray. God is woven into the intimate daily texture of her life with such thoroughness and finality that Israel has no need of the physical presence of the temple in order to pray.[9]

Praise

Her most frequent prayer is the praise of God, the Covenant God, the Creator; His power is borne witness to as all the elements of creation glorify Him, Israel herself joining the paean in honor of all creation and its God. (Cf. psalm 8, psalm 32 [33].) There is also the prayer of thanksgiving for God's intervention in her history, celebrating in hymn and liturgy His continuous care for her protection, glorification and defense. Listen, for instance, to the eloquent testimony of psalm 67 [68], psalm 75 [76], psalm 105 [106].

Then there are the prayers of petition. Because her point of view is that of this world, and she sees the cosmos as closely united to God, her prayers for material benefits are frequent; for crops at the time they are needed; for deliverance from the danger of war, persecution and calumny; for a long life and for many children. Sara prays in her ill-repute, Job in his sufferings; all Israel prays in her misfortunes, for her individual needs and for those of the nation as a whole. When besieged by hostile forces she prays for victory, and when victory comes she celebrates the victory in thanksgiving.

It would be false, however, to conclude that there is no room in Israel's thought for her spiritual needs. Moses implored Jahweh to grant him a successor to continue his work, and Solomon pleased the Lord by asking for the spiritual gift of wisdom, to govern the kingdom of Jahweh on earth in a way that might be the reflection on earth of the eternal kingship of Jahweh Himself. Again, prayer for the gift of fear of the Lord, prayer for strength to lead a virtuous life, prayer for the grace to avoid sin and to be preserved in the time of temptation are all frequent in Israel. Particularly moving is the tone of the great penitential prayers as we hear it in Nehemias 9, Daniel 9 and Esdras 9. When the Israelite has sinned he pours forth his soul to God with tears and falls prostrate to the ground, or dresses himself in mourning clothes, or rends his garments in acknowledgment of the fact that as a miserable sinner he has need of God.[10]

In the beginning no special time was set for prayer; the Israelite felt that he should approach God seven times a day—which is his way of saying that one should pray continuously. God should be the framework against which the daily activities of life are carried out. The pious Israelite prayed at least twice a day, in the morning and at night. The psalmist says that he turned to God at dawn: "In the morning I carry my cry before you" (ps. 5:4); and we know that Daniel prayed three times daily. There were also morning and evening sacrifices to which the Israelite united himself spiritually, and corporally as well if it was at all possible to be present at these sacrifices offered in the temple for the entire people. Later, in the time of Christ, it became customary to pray at the sixth and at the ninth hour.

Prayer was therefore held in the very highest esteem in Israel, from the beginning looked on as a complement to sacrifice—a sort of silent prayer in itself. It is natural for man to express petition to God together with his thanksgiving and repentance, and for these realities prayer and sacrifice are perfectly suited.

The Israelite people, as we have seen, liked to pray in the sanctuaries and to make pilgrimages to the holy places where their hearts were filled with the glory of the liturgy. One has only to read psalm 137 from verse 5 on about the Fall of Jerusalem to realize the central place that the sanctuary occupies in the life of Israel.

Exuberance and joy abound in Israel's piety because she experiences all the good things of this life, material abundance and happiness, as a revelation of God's goodness; because the world itself is seen as closely united to God. The cosmos is close to the Theos in Israel. Isaias 6:3 proclaims that the earth is filled with His glory, and that the clouds reflect Him. Therefore since the entire world represents God and reflects Him there is very little withdrawal from the world in Israel, although she does criticize the building of mighty armies, mighty cities, and, in the early period, the institution of kingship. She also criticizes the accumulation of immense fortunes or disdain for the poor. A restrained approach to highly organized urban civilization is joined to great joy in the simple things of life. There is a tendency among certain of her mystics to try to lead her to the nomadic ways of the desert; but this was never a classical theme approved by the prophets.

Eudamonism

As a result of these characteristics Israel often seems to be earthly-minded and eudaimonistic. Such an attitude is possible in the Old Testament; we would never find there a chapter such as the third in the Epistle to the Romans, which emphasizes the breach in the whole creation made by original sin, as a result of which sinful elements are everywhere, and creaturedom itself is bound to servitude and sin. Such an atmosphere would be alien to the Old Testament.

In fact, in Old Testament literature we find no full comprehension of the idea of original sin. Israel is aware of the fact that she is sinful and that she must reject sin and rid herself of it; but the idea of sinfulness latent in human nature itself is very little apparent. Israel stresses the tendency in man which leads him not to observe the Torah. But she lacks the profound conviction which Christianity has of the danger in creatures deriving from man's fall, the knowledge that creatures have departed from their original destiny to serve man and have power to harm him. Thus, as we have seen, Israel takes creatures to herself in a hearty, almost earthy manner.

God's Servant

Life is looked at from an optimistic point of view even when there are sufferings. Death is considered the end of life; and there is a this-world, this-life emphasis in all Israel's piety. Joel sees that this world will finally be destroyed; but before his time this was not a popular concept in Israelite thought. True, man is reminded by the prophets that he must have humility and that he must serve God as His *Ebed,* His servant. But the position of servant is an honorable one. Only God is holy, and before His transcendent holiness man recognizes that he is wretched, poor and a sinner. He submits fully to the will of God, but not without the exercise of his spiritual freedom in expressing his opinion of the way God is running the universe and managing life.

Moral Emphasis

In addition to all these prefigurations of grace in Israel's religious life there is also the presence of remarkable qualities in her prayer. To begin with, in order to be heard, man must be good; he must lead a life according to the testament, to the covenant, and to the demands of the law, for only the upright will be heard by God. There are, for instance, the beautiful lines from Isaias 58:8-10; "Then shall thy light break forth as the morning . . . and thy darkness shall be as the noonday." But Isaias adds that this will occur only if you have helped your neighbor in need, if you have fed the hungry and clothed the naked and redeemed captives. Then when you call Jahweh will answer you; if you cry for aid He will say: "Here I am," if you have done all these things; but you must be virtuous in order to ascend unto the mountain of Jahweh, you must have a clean heart and clean hands. He who has strayed from the path of righteousness will not be heard by God, even as Moses told the Israelites that they might weep all they liked but God would not take notice because they had not obeyed His will. And earlier, Isaias had said much the same: "Hold out your hands as you will, you shall get no heed from me; add prayer to prayer, I will not listen; are not those hands stained with blood?" (Isa. 1:15.) Clearly God accepts prayer only when it arises out of a spirit submissive to Jahweh and His will. "An unkind person who stops his ears to the poor man's cry, shall cry and get no answer" (Prov. 21:13).

Before God will hear the prayer of the Israelite he is expected to imitate the morality of God Himself, His *sedeqah* and *mishpat,* justice and judgment, and the *hesed* of God Himself. He must show reverence; to change one's clothes and to wash one's feet before entering the temple is to manifest this reverence. He must be humble, for he is, after all, but "a dust particle on a balance," "a leaf," "a dried-up stalk," a blade of grass that tomorrow will be thrown into the oven. And he must realize his utter dependence upon God, who is free to answer his prayer or not, or to postpone His answer for a time. Thus David prayed for his child, and his child died; Samuel prayed for Saul the whole night through, but his prayer did not avail; Anna asked for a child many times and made many pilgrimages, but the Lord did not grant her desire; Moses asked Jahweh to let him enter the Promised Land, but God did not allow it. Sometimes He delays and sometimes He answers the prayer in another fashion. But always God is king, His rule is sovereign, and He will choose the time of answering. Our part is to accept this, as Joel tells us.

The Israelite, of course, should never cease from praying. Judith complained because the people had set a limit to their prayer, resolving to stop if God did not deliver them within five days. Abraham's petition for a son was granted only long after it could have been humanly expected, and the Israelites asked Samuel to pray for them without ceasing; Nehemias prayed day and night for Israel.

The Notion of Corporate Personality

The Israelite is urged above all to see in God a Father who has a loving concern for him, as is evident, for instance, in psalm 3:3-5ff., psalm 9A:10-11, and psalm 12(13):6.

The great prayer-book of Israel is, of course, the book of Psalms. Now, as we have said, it is noteworthy that from the beginning Israel's approach to prayer is at once highly individualistic and highly communal. Eve prays, the Patriarchs pray, Agar prays, Abraham's servant prays, Moses and Anna pray. Each man is always part of the covenanted people, but he is also always an individual with personal responsibilities to observe the Mosaic law and to foster his individual relationship to God. Some authors have re- marked that the community after the exile seems to dissolve into a mass of individual units each going his own way, each operating independently, each responsible in a strictly individual way for his own salvation or damnation. But this is not true. The exiles were united in very many things, and when they returned they were united around the temple; for Israel was always a unified people. The source of this error may lie in part in the failure to understand the notion of corporate personality, wherein the accent shifts continually from the corporate to the individual.

Old Testament men always prayed as individuals. It is quite impossible to conceive of Mosaic legislation being given to the nation to be observed by her as a corporate entity; nations do not keep the sabbath, nor covet other nations' wives. The prophets clearly aimed at individual repentance and individual conversion, especially in the later eras, and throughout Israel's history from the beginning the individual and personal approach to God is evident in the way in which Israelite children were named. The belief that God watches over the life of each individual is crystallized in the bestowal of names like "Jahweh takes," "beloved of Jahweh," "Jahweh redeems," "Jahweh knows"; thus God was brought into relationship with the child as a patron, much as Christian children today have patron saints chosen for them.

Israel a Prefiguration of the Church

Israelite piety—at once communal and individual, deeply personal, centered above all on faith in God, who is believed to be near, to be powerful and able to understand the needs of His people—is a clear heralding of the coming of grace. For the grace of Christ is present by anticipation in Israel, prefigured in type and symbol. This people, formed by God, covenanted to Him, is itself a prefiguration of the Church of Christ. It is first of all the divine initiative which makes Israel a people. Although the ancestors of Abraham were doubtless polytheists, God chooses him to receive the revelation of His uniqueness and transcendence, of the fact that He is a living and present God, acting in history to aid the community and the individual. God will make of Israel, a people unremarkable for art or philosophy, the depository of His revelation. To Israel He has given His law. He Himself has chosen the sacrament of circumcision, the sign of the covenant, as the mark of membership of His people. The sacrifices that Israel offers are related to the unique sacrifice of the cross, and from it they draw their power to please Jahweh.

In many ways throughout the long centuries the Church is being prepared in Israel. The grace of Christ solicits man's heart through the law and the prophets. Humanity, harassed by the powers of evil, is nevertheless constantly touched, worked upon, by the grace of Christ. The flowering of Christianity is already foretold in this unique people, wholly orientated towards the kingdom of Jahweh, when the suffering servant will redeem His people from their iniquities and bear the burdens of them all. For two thousand years God instructs them by prophetic guidance, directing them towards the purest monotheism, purging prayer and rite and interior attitudes of all legalism, magic and extrinsicism. With the revelation of Himself to Israel as the saving God, the God of ineffable tenderness, of unbelievable condescension, a new world begins with Abraham, to form the setting for the redemptive incarnation. Grace continues to work in the hearts of men, within a well-defined order of religious structure, its task to form a unit which will give birth to the Church. If Israel is faithful, God will be more so, and He appeals to her again and again for faith in Him, the living and helping One. The grace of Christ saves the Israelite, because he believes in the future Redeemer, and all Israel is a divine tracing of the Mystical Body of Christ to come.[11]

NOTES

1. Rondet, *Gratia Christi*, pp. 31-38.

2. A. Lemonney, "Providence," *D.T.C.*, col. 935.

3. W. Eichrodt, *Theologie des alten Testaments* (Berlin, Evangelische Verlagsanstalt, 1950), Vol. I, pp. 110-114.

4. N. Snaith, *Distinctive Ideas of the Old Testament* (London, Epworth Press, 1957), p. 35. Cf. W. Lofthouse, "*Hen* and *Hesed* in the Old Testament, *Zeitschrift für die altestamentliche Wissenschaft* (1944), p. 30.

5. E. Jacob, *Theology of the Old Testament* (New York, Harper, 1958), p. 104.

6. T. Torrance, *The Doctrine of Grace in the Apostolic Fathers* (Edinburgh, Oliver and Boyd, 1948), p. 15.

7. Th. Vriezen, *An Outline of Old Testament Theology* (Oxford, Basil Blackwell, 1958), p. 320.

8. P. Heinisch, *Theology of the Old Testament* (Collegeville, Liturgical Press, 1955), pp. 237-241.

9. H. Lesetre, "Prière," *D.B.*, col. 665. Cf. Eichrodt, *op. cit.*, pp. 78-81.

10. A. Gelin, *The Religion of Israel* (New York, Hawthorne, 1959), pp. 44-48.

11. Journet, *op. cit.*, p. 86.

3

THE SEMANTIC
EVOLUTION OF GRACE

THE SEMANTIC EVOLUTION of the term grace is interesting because
in the New Testament there are many words which are used to
describe divine gifts; for instance, "holiness," "life in Christ,"
"eternal life," "presence," "inhabitation of the Divine Persons."
All these terms denote the mystery of the Christian existence and
the Christian mode of activity. The gifts of God and the gift of
God Himself to the human person are, however, generally expressed
today in terms of "grace," the Greek *charis*. We shall trace its evolution in the New Testament, and the evolution of its equivalent in
the Old Testament.

Charis a New Word

To begin with, we note that the choice by the new Christians of
the word "grace" (*charis*) to indicate the reality of man's divinization
is striking, for this was not a word with a long religious history
among them. To express the total newness of their experience, the
overwhelming experience of God's goodness in their Christian
life, a new word was required. One familiar with Jewish tradition
might have expected a different choice—justice, for example, or
fidelity or truth. Such words were in common use among the
prophets. The term grace itself emphasizes, in addition to the new-

ness of the Christian experience, the absolute gratuity of God's goodness to us, for the word carried this connotation throughout its history.[1]

Traditionally, as we have seen, grace has a double meaning. It is used first of all in an objective sense; for example, we say that one has sanctifying grace in his soul. We mean by this that one has an objective principle of life in his soul—not an image or a thought but an extra-mental reality. In the subjective sense, grace is the interior attitude on God's part which evokes the gift to man. It is from God's benevolence, condescension, goodness, mercy, loving-kindness that this objective gift in man's soul issues. There is need to stress this point, for in the later tradition in the Church, in so many books, and in catechism instructions it is the objective sense of grace which is emphasized, at the expense of its first meaning—the interior divine attitude which *causes* this gift.

The history of grace shows that in biblical revelation, on the contrary, it is not the objective sense which is primary but the subjective one. To separate the idea of the gift from the giver, in this case, is to arrive at an over-objectified idea of grace, as though it were a mathematical entity; whereas its effect is always to foster a dialogue between man and God as between persons. For God's love is efficacious. If even human love is capable of altering the one to whom it is directed, all the more does divine love transform its object. When God looks on man with love, He alters the very structure of man's being, producing in it, through the objective gift we call grace, a reflection of His own inner attitude of generosity, mercy and loving-kindness.

Grace always implies two liberties: the sovereign liberty of God, who is the transcendent Subject, and the liberty of man which God solicits. He invites man to a union with Him, the closest union that He can accord to man while he remains a human person. If tradition heavily underscores the objective aspect of grace, this chapter is intended to emphasize the subjective aspect, the loving-kindness of God which inspired Him to give grace.

First of all, we must note that the authors of the New Testament derived the term *charis* not directly from profane Greek literature but from the Greek translation of the Old Testament, the Septuagint. We ought, however, to examine the use of the word in profane Greek literature if we are to understand certain nuances of thought derived from it in the New Testament Greek.

In profane Greek literature the root meaning of *charis* is that which shines or glitters, which delights the eye. It can refer to corporal beauty, to the grace of personality, to art, music or poetry, to the sweetness of life—the heroism of war, the joys of marriage, of wine, of sleep, and even the grace of virtue itself.

Sometimes, too, grace is hypostatized in the notion of a goddess or goddesses of grace who pour out in our existence all that is delightful and beautiful. There is an echo of this fundamental meaning in the theological truth that man in sanctifying grace is transformed, is made supernaturally beautiful, and exercises an attractive force on God. God dwells in the man in the state of grace because man in this state draws Him irresistibly. So the gift of created grace is inseparable from the gift of Uncreated Grace.[2]

A frequently found meaning of *charis* in old Greek literature is perfection, the objective perfection of a person, which renders him charming, lovable. In profane Greek literature, this objective perfection is often corporal beauty which gives grace, charm, lovability to the one who possesses it. This meaning, for instance, is found in the *Iliad* 14:183, and in the *Odyssey* 6:237. When applied to the gods, *charis* is normally that good will and favor for which men pray and sacrifice. The gods' gifts can also be classified as graces which objectify their benevolence. Both sides of a human relationship can be described as grace if one person is generous and the other grateful.

Still another meaning of *charis* is favor, benevolence or goodness, liberality, generosity. This obviously is the more subjective meaning. It describes the inner sentiments of the superior towards the inferior; for example, the master towards his servant, or God toward His adorers. It is a disinterested goodness, but in Greek literature this goodness of the gods is not purely gratuitous, for it is provoked by the objective charm of merit or beauty of the favored one. We also find the term *charis* used in old Greek literature as the objective expression of the goodness, favor, benevolence of someone—in other words, a gift, a benefit.

Evolution in Meaning

There is a certain evolution in all this. Originally the word had one meaning; in time, however, it began to denote related ideas. Thus we find the notion of gratitude being introduced; *charis* can mean gratitude for a favor received, as well as the attitude which provoked the favor. In Hellenistic Greek most of the classical meanings of grace continue and new ones are added. At times the joy suggested by the word comes to be identified with pleasure, or even lust. It is frequently employed for an object, endowment or gift from the gods. It receives, too, a deepening of its psychological overtones and is more often associated with friendship and good will. The good will, the condescension of the gods, is a frequent usage. As the gods show good will, so may the emperor, and as the emperor is divinized royal favor comes to have also a religious significance. Grace becomes, not only a kindly act on the part of the Caesar, but an immortal and divine attribute of the Caesar. The divine power that dwells within the ruler issues in acts of gracious condescension. In its later stages of evolution in Hellenistic Greek prose, grace assumes the character of a mystical power, a super-human quality bringing charm, prosperity, influence.

There are two special uses of *charis* in ancient Greek literature worthy of note. First, it denotes the favors the emperor would accord to his soldiers; these were called "charities." On the emperor's birthday, or on New Year's day, he gave sums of money to the soldiers; the word used to describe that money was *charis*. Because the emperor was not forced to give, the idea of pure gratuity is underscored. (The same notion will be pointed out later when we consider grace as God's gift to man.)

Secondly, *charis* is used to mean a certain internal power by which one is able to perform marvellous things. One finds this idea echoed in St. Paul's use of the term and particularly in the Acts of the Apostles. The Acts are called "the gospel of the Holy Spirit," because they record the presence of the Spirit in the young Christian community and the manifestation of marvellous powers and gifts which accompany the Spirit. The same idea is implied in what we call charisms, gifts given not for personal sanctification but for the community; for example, the gift of languages.

In the Old Testament, the Hebrew root which is usually translated in Greek by *charis* is *hen*. When used in the physical sense it means to lean over someone, to bend over and watch someone, a notion echoed in the idea that the Spirit broods over the waters of baptism. In the moral sense, in the mental sense, it conveys the idea of "bending over" with favor, kindness, benevolence, protection, love, as when the mother bends over the cradle. In this sense it can be used to refer to the favor of God.

In the historical books, the earliest books of the Old Testament, the word we translate as grace means the favor which the inferior finds, or hopes to find, in the eyes of his superior, Jahweh; for example, Abraham found "grace" with God; Moses found "grace" with God; that is, God regarded them with favor and benevolence. Esther, in the Book of Esther (8:5) possibly found grace with King Assuerus. All the early books of the Old Testament are the history of the *charis* of Jahweh: the grace, favor and benevolence of Jahweh toward the prophets and patriarchs. Early Hebrew history is the story of the invasion of God into Jewish history through His love for this people. He has chosen this people and He will make it His own.[3]

The prophets rarely used this word. One finds it only twice in a religious sense. Jeremias uses it in 31:2, where the people who had escaped from the sword found grace in the desert; that is, they found favor or benevolence from God, for they had escaped from the sword. In Zacharias 12:10, one finds the expression, "I will spread abroad a disposition of goodness and prayer"; here the notion is a spirit of goodness. The Book of Proverbs uses *hen* (*charis*) several times in the sense of physical charm or beauty; for example, 1:9; 4:9; the psalms use it twice, psalm 44 [45]:3 and psalm 83 [84]:12, in both of which cases it means the favor or goodness of God. The Book of Wisdom uses it six times; in Wisdom 3:9 it means a recompense, in 14:26 it means gratitude for a benefit; in 18:2 it means pardon. The last books of the Old Testament generally stress the sense of benefit. When the word *charis* is used in a religious sense (beauty, charm, amiability do not carry religious connotations), it ordinarily means divine favor, or, occasionally, the merciful, gratuitous goodness of God—the condescension of Jahweh, the source of all our blessings.[4]

The Gospels and Acts

It is clear, therefore, that the Old Testament or classical Greek meaning of *charis* gave no suggestion of the great future it would have in Christianity. It was a word typically Greek in spirit—the notion of amiability, lovability, based on corporal charm and beauty. Nor did it have in the Old Testament a sharply defined religious sense. In fact, as we have said, the Old Testament had many other words which it preferred to *charis* in order to express God's relationship to the individual soul. Justice and judgment, the Hebrew *sedeqah* and *mishpat,* are more favored words. Truth and fidelity, goodness and tenderness, *hesed* (goodness) are often used. The prophets Micheas and Amos speak almost exclusively of justice when they write of what we would express by the term grace. Osee uses goodness and tenderness, *hesed we rehamim.* The first Isaias speaks mainly of truth, and second Isaias of justice and salvation.

All these terms—truth, justice, salvation, goodness and tenderness —are salvaged and used again in the New Testament. We find in St. Paul, for example, all the terms used by the prophets; nevertheless they are very often replaced by the new term, *charis*. The evangelists—Matthew, Mark, Luke and John—did not make this change. John chose the word *agape*, or love, to underscore the fact that grace is the result of an inner attitude on the part of God towards the individual. *Charis* is totally lacking in Matthew and in Mark, the two evangelists who think more in Old Testament terms. One finds the word *charis* eight times in the Gospel of Luke and seventeen times in the Acts. It is never found on the lips of Our Lord, apparently because it was not in the vocabulary of the times. Since He was speaking to the Jews, He used the terms with which they were familiar, the prophetical images of salvation, justice and truth.[5]

In St. John's prologue one finds the word *charis* used three times. We read in 1:14, ". . . and the Word was made flesh and dwelt amongst us; we have contemplated His glory, the glory which the Father gives to His unique Son, full of grace and of truth." Grace here probably expresses the divine attribute of benevolence and of love, and the objective expression in Christ of God's goodness and benevolence. Thus Christ is regarded as the concrete embodiment of the inner goodness and mercy of God towards us. This same usage will be found later in St. Paul. In John 1:16 we read: "From his fullness, we have all received grace upon grace, for the law was given by Moses, but grace and truth have come through Jesus Christ." The Vulgate says "grace after grace"—which means that Jesus Christ is the new grace, the new favor of God, substituted for the old grace which was the law. It also implies again that the new grace manifests a special benevolence: Christ as the objectivization of the benevolence of God towards us. Thus the whole of God's attitude towards man, His redemptive mercies towards man, are summed up in an historical person. He is come as a Saviour, constituted a Redeemer by His very being as the God-man. As man

He is one of us, and as man He is capable of offering a total sacrifice and adequate satisfaction to Himself, as God, to the Father and the Holy Spirit, to redeem us from our sins. If the term *charis* is rare in St. John, the equivalent term, love, is not.

In the Gospel of St. Luke, *charis* occurs significantly four times in the Old Testament sense: the favor of God. In Luke 1:28-30, for example, the Greek means "you have been graced" before God —Mary has been graced before God. This means that Mary has found favor with God and that the favor has been expressed in the divine maternity. The use of the perfect tense indicates the stability of Mary's perfection of grace; it suggests that the grace was there from the beginning. We also notice here the use of the vocative, "Thou hast been graced"; it is actually the name God applies to Mary. In 2:40, we read that "the grace of God rested upon Him"; this means the favor of God, the benevolence and kindness and benignity of God. In 2:52 it signifies favor: Christ grew in favor with men; perhaps it also means here the sense of amiability, lovableness, charm, which the young Christ manifested as He grew up.

St. Luke has also used the word grace in the Acts of the Apostles. In 6:8, for example, we find Stephen described as full of grace and power. Stephen manifests the characteristic power which grace gives. In Acts 11:23, we are told that Barnabas seized the grace of God; that is, that he seized the manifestations and the fruits of grace, the conversion of the pagans, their entry into Christianity and into the Church; this *is* the power of grace being manifested for him. In Acts 13:43 we find Paul and Barnabas exhorting the Jews to remain faithful to the grace of God—that is, to remain faithful to the word of salvation, which is a person, Christ Jesus, and to the justification which God has given them, not through the law but through faith in Christ Jesus. Grace is identical here with faith or with Christianity. Paul urges the Jews to remain constant to the faith, adhering to Christianity, and being devoted to the grace of God, the goodness of God. They must realize that faith comes to them also as a gift, a grace from God.

In Acts 15:11, one observes a new nuance, specifically Pauline. The text stresses the fact that grace is salvific. This is the characteristic Pauline notion of the healing effect of grace later taken up by St. Augustine, and as we have said, it is one of two traditional approaches to grace. One group looks on grace as the divinization of the Christian—this is the oriental or Greek way. The Latin, Augustinian or Pauline, approach is to see the grace of God as something needed for a good moral life. Both approaches are orthodox. The question here is one of emphasis. It is the person of Jesus Christ, revealing God's love in redemptive action, who is the source of the gospels' position on grace. While the word is infrequently used in the gospels, and when used can generally be explained in a non-distinctive sense, the reality of grace is present throughout as the action of God revealed in Christ. His person and work declare the gospel meaning of grace more adequately than the word.

The entirely singular event recounted by the four evangelists, the entrance of God into human history, objectively accomplished in Jesus Christ, dominates the gospel account of man's relationship with God. This relationship can no longer be adequately expressed as a mere fulfillment of divine command. The entire outlook of man is altered by the fact of the Incarnation, the final self-commitment of God, anticipated in the covenant. Christ Himself is the objective content of grace in its distinctive Christian meaning. Because of this connection with the person of Christ, God's self-disclosure and self-donation, the concept of grace in the gospels marks an utterly new development, quite unexpected, as we have observed, in view of its semantic roots.

The teaching of Christ concerning the merciful love of the Father is entirely a commentary on the grace of the Father. It is the initiative of divine love that is brought home repeatedly to the listener. The prodigal son, the lost groat, the lost sheep show forth the spontaneous love of the Father. The commandment to love thy

neighbor "as thyself"—not at all a limiting phrase in Hebrew thought
—echoes this same revelation of unconditioned love, freely given. It
is in Christ's own redemptive activity of healing, His compassion,
His mercy and forgiveness that we encounter grace. He Himself
identified the spontaneous love of Jahweh with His own person.
The redemptive intentions of the Godhead are actualized in His
person, and Jesus' consciousness of this is evident. His invitation
is to drink of living waters; He is the light of the world, the way,
the truth and the life. The longings and aspirations of Isaias are
fulfilled in Him. The covenant-love of God has become embodied
in His person, so that the eternal is not only revealed and proclaimed
by Him but is embodied in Him. The salvific justice of God has
realized its final initiative, independently of man's sinfulness, in His
sinless self.

Jesus deliberately confronted Israel with the accomplishment of
God's saving initiative in Himself and proclaimed Himself the only
way to the Father, for the Father and He are one. It is impossible
for man to approach the Father save through Him, and merely
human effort, mere human observance of command, cannot be
the basis for human hope. Man's relationships with God are determined by the position he assumes in relation to the living Christ
who identifies Himself with God's forgiving and justifying action.
The entire viewpoint of Christianity is at stake here. All notions of
a purely forensic justification, of purely human merit, disappear; it
is personal loyalty to the One whose initiative is utterly primary
that is required. Jesus' identification of grace with His own person
is what places Him at the center of Christian piety. Men approach
in Him the living and holy God who intends to redeem and who
anticipates man's response with His freely given self-commitment.

In Christ Jesus the ineffable love of God for the world has broken
into human history in such a way as to set the Christian life on a
new basis. Grace has received its fulfillment in Him. Ethical, moral
and religious life from now on have found their aim. The salvific
act has taken place in Him. He is our Pasch, and in Him God's

justice and love have invaded human life in an entirely new way. If the word grace is rare in the gospels, its meaning is present wherever the name of Jesus is mentioned—that Jesus in whom God makes the definitive gracious movement to man.

St. Paul

In Pauline writings the word grace occurs more than twice as often as in the other New Testament writers combined. It is also interesting to note the situations in which it occurs. There are more than twenty-one references to grace in the Epistle to the Romans, and more than twelve in the Epistle to the Ephesians, the two Pauline syntheses on grace. Occasionally we encounter the word *charis* with the signification of charm, amiability, lovability, as in Galatians 4:6, where we are told that our language should be charming and attractive. Grace also indicates human benefit, and we read of the collection taken up to support the Church of Jerusalem. Again, we find *charis* as a synonym for what we would call charism—a grace given for the apostolate rather than for one's personal sanctification. Romans 12:6 and Ephesians 4:7 have this meaning of the word. St. Paul also uses the term for the particular vocation which he himself received in the apostolate (1 Cor. 3:10). The fundamental senses in which St. Paul uses the terms, however, are: first, grace is gratuitous; second, it is the favor of God and of Christ, merciful and liberal, which pardons sins and causes us to overflow with divine benefits. St. Paul's greetings at the beginning and at the conclusion of his epistles are also significant. "May the grace and peace of Christ be with you—grace and peace of Christ and our Father and Lord. The grace of our Lord, Jesus Christ, the love of God and the communion of the Holy Spirit be with you." In Paul, the terms "grace of God" and "grace of Christ" have slightly different meanings. He writes, for example, in 1 Cor. 1:4, "I do not cease to render thanks to God with regard to you, for the grace of God which has been given you through Christ Jesus." This implies the merciful love of the Eternal Father—the subjective sense of grace objectified in the person of Christ, who is the benefit this love gives. In Galatians 1:15, where we read that the grace of God calls the Apostle Paul and has the effect of revealing the Son to him, we are again presented with the merciful love of God calling Paul, the objective effect of which call is to reveal Christ to him. Paul's thought keeps moving from the Eternal Father to the Son; when he speaks of the Father, it is usually the interior, subjective aspect of grace that is objectified in Christ Jesus. Christ *is* our grace, so to speak. In Romans 3:24 we read, "you are all justified gratuitously by grace," that is to say, by the goodness of God, and this goodness divinizes. In 2 Tim. 1:8-9 Paul writes, "Suffer with me for the gospel, sustained by the power of God who has saved us and called us to a holy vocation, not because of our works but because of his own proper plan and of his grace," or, as it can be read, "because of His own gracious plan." Here the word gracious conveys the note of benignity and goodness. This grace has been given from eternity in Christ Jesus. In the eternal plan of God the grace that we receive today has been given in the light of Jesus Christ, because of Him who is predestined to be the Saviour. It has been manifested, this grace, in our Lord; He is the epiphany of the goodness of God, the manifestation of God's benignity, so that one could say that the Incarnation and the Redemption are the manifestation of grace, or grace entered in human history, the historical embodiment of God's love in Christ Jesus.[6]

In St. Paul, then, grace is essentially the gracious design of God to save all men. It is always redemptive. Just as Paul's preoccupations are almost always soteriological, salvific and redemptive, his theology a vast tract on the Redemption. From all eternity, this gracious plan of God is present in the eternal Word, and when He appears it is given concrete manifestation, so that one can say that Christ the Redeemer is incarnate grace, the incarnate love of God. In the new dispensation, law has been superseded, and a principle of activity which we call grace, identical with love, has been made *the* law of Christianity. Augustine's "Love and do what you will" is now theologically defensible.

"Through Jesus Christ we have access by faith to that grace in which we stand" (Rom. 5:12). Grace here is equivalent to the whole realm of Christianity to which we come through Jesus Christ. Grace is, it seems, our homeland, our *patria*, an atmosphere in which we live and move and have our being.

In St. Paul, then, we see the essential meaning of grace as the gratuitous favor of God especially manifest in the economy of the redemption. The accent is on the subjective inner love of God thus manifesting itself in His gratuitous and independent choice to redeem mankind in Christianity. We do, however, find the objective sense in St. Paul. He refers, for example, to Christ as grace, Christianity as grace, the realm of faith as grace; the interior gift which the Christian possesses as grace, and the power which he possesses to do salvific acts as grace. But the major emphasis is subjective, and it is always used in the singular. There is only one major grace, and that is the love of God which gives us Christ. There is only one interior attitude, love: and there is only one gift, the Christ.

St. Paul insists strongly on the notion that grace is freely given. For him, there arises in the heart of God a love for man which is not a response to lovability on man's part but which creates lovability in man. God hardens the hearts of those whom He will, and He has mercy upon whom He will. In the Augustinian theology, which follows that of St. Paul, the notion of gratuity is also stressed. Occasionally, however, this question arises in St. Augustine: grace is freely given by God; could He perhaps have given more? This is the question of predestination, but it does not arise for Paul; for him grace is not measured out mathematically. Grace is the milieu in which we live and move and have our being; it is the divine atmosphere in which we breathe, for God is always present in His gifts. He does not send them as an absent friend; He comes personally, making Himself really, dynamically present in the soul, united to it in a union whose intimacy is surpassed only by that of the hypostatic union. To Paul it would have been difficult to think in terms of more or less when God has clearly given us so much. His notion of the gratuity of grace came from the realization that even the Gentile might be saved, that others besides Jews were destined for salvation in the plan of God. If the Gentile, who certainly had no merits in Jewish eyes, was called to salvation, then obviously grace was independent of works. For St. Paul grace was a new word which would express a tremendous event, the coming of Christ; it was the word which expresses the whole of Christianity, the law of love, the law of liberality, the law of grace.

We are fairly certain, as we have said, that the word was adopted to express an experience which the Christian community knew was unparalleled in history. Indeed the fact that this word is lacking in the gospels gives evidence of their authenticity, for the experience was not communal at the time they were written and was not, properly speaking, part of the evangelical message. It seems rather a theological word which belongs to faith at a definite stage of its development.

Paul also comes to the notion of gratuity from the idea that we are sinners in need of redemption. As sinners we can make no claims on the divine goodness; and yet the divine goodness bends over us and gives us the Christ. Again, we are sinners, and yet by grace we claim friendship from God. But all friendship is free; we can never say that we have rights to another person's friendship, or claim it as a debt. Friendship is a meeting of two liberties. Since all human friendship is gratuitous, how much more so is a friendship between a creature and God? The friendship we claim is that of a divine person, and it is obvious that this must be free, since it is impossible for a creature to lay claim to friendship with God.

It is this gratuity of grace which distinguishes Christianity to a large extent from all pagan religions. In paganism it was believed that through certain magical formulas one could force the gods to grant favors. As we have seen, the Greeks of antiquity generally held that God Himself was impersonal. To Aristotle, Plato, Plotinus it would be inconceivable that the gods should respond to the worshiper with any resonance of personal friendship or love, for they were incapable of either. So this idea that God Himself turns toward us with a favor which is infinite, and that He loves us, is wholly new. It is an idea which permeates St. Paul and St. John, and the Holy Spirit does not choose words carelessly. Such words as love, *agape,* and *charis* are chosen because they are the most apt to designate the interior reality in God.

Ephesians 2:8 speaks of the "gratuitous favor of God," and Hebrews 4:16 reads: "Let us then approach with confidence to the throne of grace." In Hebrews 10:29 we are asked not to outrage the Holy Spirit, not to outrage the spirit of grace. The author of Hebrews uses the expression "the spirit of grace" for any one of three reasons: because in the Holy Spirit all the lesser graces God gives us are concentrated, because the Holy Spirit is the substantial love within the Trinity, or because the Holy Spirit is the one who assures us of the love, the *gratia,* the favor of God. The Spirit assures us of the love of God by crying out with ineffable groanings within us, "Abba, Father." He inspires us to call God the Father, our Father, the source of benedictions and goodness.

In Hebrews 12:15 we are told to watch that no root of bitterness, springing up, should deprive us of the grace of God. In Hebrews 13:9 grace is shown as lending stability to the heart, which in biblical terminology, particularly in the Old Testament, is the symbol of the whole interior life. The inner life finds its stability and strength, not in exterior practices, not in observance of the law, but in grace, the divine favor. It is God's goodness bending over our weakness which lends us continuity and stability in our effort to give ourselves to Him.

"Grace and peace be yours abundantly," says St. Peter (1 Peter 1:2). The salvation announced by the prophets, grace, is in the sufferings and in the glory of Christ. Grace here is identified with the salvation announced by the prophets, because Christ is the new grace who takes the place of the old law and the prophets.

We read in 1 Peter 5:12; "I have written to you exhorting and testifying that this is the true grace of God. Stand firmly in it." This true grace of God is the Christian religion, the new religion in which the Christian has been established and rendered firm. This is the true, the lasting, the final revelation of God in Christ. "Stand firm," says St. Paul in another place, "hold the traditions you have learned" (2 Thess. 2:14).

The absolutely gratuitous initiative of God in Christ overwhelmed Paul on the road to Damascus, producing in the ultimate reaches of his soul the realization that the condescension of God is no response to human merit, and his experience of this grace of the risen Christ was to hold him enthralled for the rest of his life. For until that moment had he not been actively engaged in persecuting the Church of Christ? What Paul could not forget was the merciful gesture of the living Christ in reaching out His hand to pluck him free of the imprisoning zeal of Phariseeism. And this free election of Christ is further confirmed by an appointment as Apostle to the Gentiles. Little wonder, then, that Paul's concept of grace—and to him the word is a technical term—is never wholly separated from the figure of Christ! Christ had graciously bestowed upon Paul His gift of a new life, and the very circumstances in which He did so threw into relief the notions of gratuity and personal love. In his thought the doctrine of grace will always be closely allied to the person of Christ, in whom God has accomplished our salvation through the folly of the cross, the source of grace.

Grace a Key-Word

Paul will make of grace, as opposed to law, one of the key-words to the basic message of the new revelation. To Paul there is no complete separation between the new life given by Christ, the work

He accomplished, and His divine self. The cross, the risen Christ, the ineffable love of the Father, the gift of the Spirit and the new life of grace are all closely connected. Christ risen is God's powerful grace among men, and His gifts are inseparable from Himself and His work of redemption. It is the gift of God to men in Christ's sacrifice of the cross that is the very heart of the meaning of the created gift of grace. What it does is to establish something radically new, surpassing even a new law; it is a new life, communicated to us from Christ. Grace in St. Paul discloses a new perspective which puts man's relationship to God in a new light, altering the understanding of history itself and revealing the love of God for man in a way impossible before Christ.[7]

It is important to realize that for Paul grace is not something merely similar to divine mercy which comes to the rescue of man and helps him to lead a life conformed to moral law. It is not something which merely aids man's self-effort at morality, although it does this also, but it is something which primarily constitutes man's life on an entirely new foundation. Grace elevates him to the divine order. Grace is the basic presupposition of the entire Christian life, not merely one of its principles. As W. Manson has said: "Grace in its primary and fundamental sense must not be conceived like the Jewish idea of the divine mercy, as something merely ancillary, something which merely comes to the assistance of man in his own efforts for righteousness. Rather is grace the will of God to constitute man's life afresh on a wholly new basis and in a renewed world, to set him free from sin and Satan; to endue him with the Spirit, to make him the possessor of a super-natural life."[8]

The love of God for men actualized itself in Jesus Christ. That same love takes hold of men and produces grace in them, becoming in them the principle of a new life. Although remaining a gift of God, it is within man, for the redeeming purpose of God lays hold of men as it laid hold of Paul, and transforms them internally. It introduces them into a new order so that they are "in the grace of

Christ," and it is in them as the source of Christian life and status. But as often as Paul reflects upon grace as a power acting on man and within him, he never loses sight of its transcendent source. Grace is from Another, and only through personal attachment to that Other, Jesus Christ, can grace come to man and be possessed as a gift flowing from His self-giving. The effect of Christ's redeeming action is an inner quality in the Christian that manifests God's free love for him.

NOTES

1. J. Guillet, *Themes of the Bible* (Notre Dame, Indiana; Fides, 1960), pp. 20-21. Cf. J. Moffat, *Grace in the New Testament* (New York, Ray Long and Richard Smith, Inc.), pp. 21-36.

2. W. T. Whitley, ed., *The Doctrine of Grace* (London, Student Christian Movement Press, 1932); see W. Manson, "Grace in the New Testament," pp. 34-36.

3. Torrance, *The Doctrine of Grace*, pp. 1-6. Cf. J. Moulton and G. Milligan, *The Vocabulary of the Greek Testament* (London, Hodder and Stoughton, 1946), article on *charis*.

4. Guillet, *op. cit.*, p. 21. Cf. C. Ryder Smith, *The Bible Doctrine of Grace* (London, Epworth Press, 1956), p. 9. Cf. also ch. 3, *passim*.

5. Guillet, *op. cit.*, p. 23.

6. P. Bonnetain, "Grâce," *Dictionnaire de la Bible, Supplément*, T. III, cols. 701-716.

7. Torrance, *op. cit.*, p. 29.

8. Manson, art. cit., p. 46.

4

GRACE IN THE FATHERS AND SCHOLASTICS

THE DOCTRINE OF GRACE received further development in the primitive and the medieval Church. We may begin with the early Fathers, although sufficient research has not yet been done on them. The *didache*, Clement of Rome, Ignatius of Antioch, Polycarp, Barnabas, Pastor Hermas, instead of the word *charis*, frequently use the word *pneuma* (spirit). Their stress is one of an interior principle of Christian *morality*. Consequently the word *charis* appears in a sense foreign to that of St. Paul, frequently indicating the natural gifts, graces, and favors which God has bestowed upon man. Still, there is no need to divorce this meaning completely from the Pauline meaning. The first gift that God grants man is existence, his own nature, temperament and endowments. These are graces in a wide sense because all are included in the divine plan to bring man to salvation. God's grace does not attach itself to man's nature as something utterly foreign to that nature or personality but comes to him as he is, congruously.[1]

The Fathers

In the early Fathers, *charis* and *pneuma* generally denote the objective idea of grace, the real, concrete gift implanted in man's soul. *Charis* usually accents the gratuity of the gift, and *pneuma* its supernatural character, the fact that it is a participation in the divine life.[2]

Irenaeus, the first great theologian, employs the word *charis* very rarely. This is astonishing, because he very carefully bases himself upon Sacred Scripture. There are many places where we would expect to find mention of *charis* but do not, and when he does use it (it is not one of his central concepts) its meaning is not sharply defined. His preference is for such terms as "divine heredity," "divine life," "divine justice," "divine glory," "adoption." Occasionally, *charis* means liberality, or munificence. In general, it has a more objective sense, but it is so vague and so global in its meaning that we cannot depend very much upon it.

Athanasius, a very distinctive and speculative theologian, uses *charis* in a somewhat unusual sense: the order or the economy of grace, that new economy which came with Christ, the new global world order set in motion by God in Christ. Occasionally it means a free gift; more often it means participation in the eternal Word, since to Athanasius this is the way in which we are deified, and we first share in the incorruptibility of God. Although he does not exclude from his notion of incorruptibility the idea of a divine image or participation in the divine nature, he stresses rather the fact that by nature the Eternal Word is incorruptible. This is, for the Word, the natural situation, and to this He has now been restored. Since we are united in Him, the more natural situation of the Christian is to be enjoying heaven, impassible and incorruptible. Christianity is always anticipating this normal situation. When man is baptized, he is baptized into the death and into the resurrection of Christ, so that he is already risen from the dead in Christ, already passed through the mystery of death in Christ. The Christian, too, has died to death, to Satan, to sin. Christ is not merely a single individual but One who incorporates all of us mystically in Himself. Therefore, we are in principle already risen from death, from sin; have already conquered gloriously even though still in a passible state. There is, however, a period of waiting. The gifts man lost through original sin are all restored to him in fact or in hope, but he must wait for the condition of death before they come to fulfillment. The Christian is already numbered among the saints; he is one whose vocation is in heaven, whose conversation should be in heaven, a member of Christ, objectively redeemed.[3]

To Athanasius, then, divinization is primarily a share in the incorruptibility of God. This is a special viewpoint, not that common to subsequent tradition. Today we say that man shares in God's nature and because of this will one day be incorruptible. Obviously, in the thought of Athanasius a certain primacy is given to the resurrection of the body.

Cyril of Alexandria uses the term *charis* very frequently, often in the subjective sense of the benevolence of God which justifies us. He uses it also to mean what we call today "the grace of the Head." Christ is sanctified in His humanity for us; He is the repository of all graces for the entire mystical body. He possesses the grace of the Head, and Christians receive their grace from Him. What we find stressed in Cyril of Alexandria is this: the prime grace received is the Holy Spirit. It is the Uncreated Grace, the presence of the divinity itself. This divine person comes to impress Himself upon the soul, to unite Himself to the soul, and in so doing produces sanctifying grace. It is as if one had a seal with a rose cut in it. The seal itself would be the Holy Spirit, the wax would be one's soul, the rose-image which arises in the wax would be created grace. By His self-donation or self-communication, by sharing what He has, God causes in man the created entity we call sanctifying grace. The Greek Fathers insist that there is no possibility of created grace in the soul unless the Holy Spirit Himself is present. The kind of causality on the part of God is that which takes place when God gives Himself. Grace is such a unique entity that it could not be produced by the ordinary causality of God. It is something sublime, not only an image of the very nature of God but a share in it.[4]

Among the Latin Fathers, the first author to mention *charis* or grace is Tertullian. He uses it to mean divine power, or *pneuma*. In the Latin Fathers, grace becomes an interior motion from God to the soul by which He orders or directs man to eternal life. What is stressed here is not so much the Pauline notion of *charis* as the Pauline notion of *pneuma*—a spirit, a force, an élan by which God directs and draws man to eternal life. This shift in emphasis is explained by the fact that the Christian community had come to a greater realization of the role of the Holy Spirit in man's sanctification. Once understood as the Holy Spirit acting within man, ordering him to holiness, grace is easily seen as a divine action interior to the soul, driving it towards a holy vision of God—eternity.

The Latin Fathers put much stress upon actual grace. To the Latins, grace becomes a medicinal agent which heals the wounds of nature and enables man one day to possess God. This action within man will cure concupiscence and enable him to observe the law of God. St. Augustine will render classic this concept of grace as a force, a power, a vigor within the soul.

To the Greek, grace was primarily elevating; it deified man; to the Latin, grace is primarily health-giving or medicinal, enabling man to lead a good moral life. This is the beginning of the great division of emphasis in the Christian Church; the Latin Church will always place great stress on the juridical and the moral in every sphere of theology, while the Greeks will always emphasize the divine gifts and the mystical. Implicit in this divinization is a dynamism which preserves it in being.

These are two ways of saying the same thing; but one must not interpret grace as a purely moral assistance. At this period in history, neither Latin nor Greek clearly distinguished between habitual grace and actual grace. The distinction was not clear even in the earlier works of St. Thomas. Christian theologians were aware that God divinized man at baptism and also that He gave an interior principle of action, helping him when needed. But the theoretical basis for a real distinction between actual grace and habitual grace was not elaborated, since there did not yet exist a philosophy of habit. It required St. Thomas, working upon the categories of Aristotle, to give us the philosophical tools by which we could explore the data of revelation in terms of philosophy. Reading the documents of the Council of Carthage and the Council of Orange, one finds it hard to determine whether they are discussing sanctifying or actual grace.

The Scholastics

With the scholastics, we arrive at a greater systemization of concepts. Earlier theologians had been dependent upon Plato and Plotinus. After Aristotle had been translated, the theologians exploited him not only as philosophers but as theologians. One of his concepts into which they delved is the category of habit; others are motion, disposition, formal effect. It is at this point in the thirteenth century, when the concepts of nature and supernature were precisely defined, that the nature of grace becomes particularly clear. St. Thomas made the distinction, and he made it because he was an Aristotelian.

The scholastics strongly emphasize the objective nature of grace. In them there is less mention of grace as divine love, the divine mercy, God Himself leaning over man in a dialogue relationship. Instead there is an insistence upon the fact that grace is a reality within the soul. The mystery, the divine penumbra, the suggestions of infinity which are, so to speak, the climate of the doctrine, are less attractive to the penetrating and analytic Latin mind than to the mystical Greek. In Latin theology God's divine benevolence and goodness are His will for man's salvation. Unfortunately, in later centuries the clarity of the Latin analysis became clouded by controversies on predestination in which God's love was insufficiently stressed. As a result, even today certain souls are terrified when they contemplate that most glorious of all God's revelations, His love for us and the mystery of predestination.

The scholastic period developed, too, the notion of merit. The interior action of God upon the soul not only cures man of his weakness and allows him to lead a good moral life, it elevates him so that he can merit before God. However, it would be a mistake to push the juridical notion of merit too far, for the very principle by which man merits is a gift from God—grace. The Latins pointed out, too, that grace is not due to man, and this on two accounts: first, because man is a sinner; secondly, because it is above the demands of nature. Now that the theologians possessed a philosophic concept of nature, the superiority of grace to nature could be discussed within a philosophic framework. Thus, there emerge for the first time with luminous clarity ideas on the supernatural quality of grace. To all primitive Christians grace was supernatural simply because it was divine, a gift from God. Sinful man had no right to it because it was God's friendship, and friendship is always something freely given. These are the terms in which the early Greek Fathers talked of the supernaturality of grace.

The Latins discuss it in quite different terms. Grace is not due to one's nature for three reasons: first, it does not constitute one's nature, it is not a part of one's nature; one can be fully a man without grace. Secondly, grace is not due to nature in the sense that it flows from nature. If one has an intellect, it is perfectly normal that occasionally one thinks; this flows naturally from the intelligence. But grace does not flow naturally from anything human— either from intellect or will or from the body. Thirdly, grace is not necessary for man to function as a man; there is a conceivable, although not a real, term to man's life possible to him without grace, namely human happiness. The Latins give much attention to another point: the stability of grace, the permanent gift which is the beginning of eternal life. Of this more will be said in the next chapter.

NOTES

1. Torrance, *The Doctrine of Grace in the Apostolic Fathers*, pp. 133-141.
2. Moffat, *Grace in the New Testament*, pp. 373-391.
3. R. Bernard, *L'Image de Dieu d'après saint Athanase* (Paris, Aubier, 1952), pp. 141-146; cf. A. de Bovis, *De Gratia Christi* (Enghein, 1952), pp. xii-xvi.
4. L. Janssens, "Notre filiation divine d'après S. Cyrille d'Alexandrie, *Ephemerides theologicae lovanienses* (1938), pp. 232-278. Cf. H. du Manoir, *Dogme et Spiritualité chez S. Cyrille d'Alexandrie* (Paris, Vrin, 1944), pp. 420-424.

II

THE CATHOLIC DOCTRINE

5

THE BEING OF GRACE

As WE HAVE SEEN, the Fathers of the early Church did not use the expression sanctifying grace, and in the early Middle Ages theologians referred to the gift itself as the grace that makes one pleasing to God. The term in this sense was gradually extended to include both actual and sanctifying grace, and the distinction between them was not worked out with clarity until the time of St. Thomas. Once the distinction was made, a new term was necessary, and sanctifying grace was settled upon.

A Formal Principle

Sanctifying grace, or the grace of the just, is not a mere extrinsic favor of God but a permanent created gift inhering in the soul. It can be defined as a formal principle of justification. A form is a kind of quality, an accident that modifies the substance in which it inheres. Thus redness qualifies a book and makes the book red; it is an accident inhering in the substance, and it is hence an intrinsic accidental form. Similarly, grace is a form inhering in the soul; it modifies the soul and renders it "such."

Obviously, when man receives grace, it is not God who changes; it is man who is qualified, who receives a new mode of existence. Sanctifying grace is not Uncreated. It is distinct from the Holy Spirit, who is also given to the soul, but not distinct in a manner excluding relationship to the Holy Spirit. There is an intrinsic and essential connection between the presence of sanctifying grace and the presence of the Holy Spirit. God, when He indwells, confers sanctifying grace; grace is the result of this inhabitation and is at the same time its condition.

A Physical Gift

Grace is moreover a physical gift. It is in the ontological order—the order of being, existence—and not in the moral order, as is the content of a thought, a decision, or an affection. To say that it is physical is to oppose it to a moral or juridical entity. By grace man is changed in the physical order. As a result of this change, man is committed to change himself in the ethical order, in the cognitive order and in the juridical order. Grace itself, however, is not in any of these orders but in that more fundamental order which we have called ontological. A meritorious act is at once a moral and an ontological reality.

Many people find difficulty in understanding the Church's insistence on the fact that grace is in the physical order, because they feel that the most important thing is a change in the moral order. Surely, they argue, there can be no more important relationship to God than a moral one. The order of thought is, however, less than the order of being. By the physical order we mean that which has extra-mental existence, that which exists outside the mind. In this sense a thing which is physical can be either spiritual or material; each of these qualities shares this characteristic: existence outside the mind. Man's soul, for example, is physical and spiritual. Mental or moral being, however, does not have the richness, the fullness, the density of extra-mental being. The idea of a good dinner does not have the fullness, the flavor, the density, the attraction of a good dinner, nor has it the nourishing value. If one ceases to think about an extra-mental being, it does not disappear from existence, for it is not dependent upon one's thought in order to exist. Neither does it exist in the moral or intentional order. A thing can exist in the moral order only if it is supported by a mind thinking or willing it. We have, then, to examine the grade of being in which this form, sanctifying grace, is placed.

The lowest grade of being is unreal being, being which cannot be real under any circumstances—for instance, a square circle. This cannot be real because it is a contradiction. God could not produce it by His omnipotence because He would be producing nothing. Although man can consider it as though it were being, to do so he has to employ two concepts, for it cannot be grasped in one. It is an "unthinkable" being. Since it cannot be thought of as one, it cannot be made as one, its notes intrinsically contradicting each other. This being is of no importance except to the logician.

Logical beings exist only in one's mind; for example, a purple cow. The idea of a purple cow is not self-contradictory, but such a being is not found in the order of nature. God could make one if He would, but so far He has not done so. Although it may have the reality of a painting, it does not have the reality of a cow; it cannot be milked.

One comes next to the notion of mental being, strictly so called; for example, my thought of man. This is something that can exist. We do not, however, expect a thought to show vitality; the thought of an orange or of an apple is quite different from the apple or the orange itself. A thought exists, but only within the mind. Therefore to be—to exist—it is dependent always on another being. This grade of being, then, is in the moral order, the juridical order, the mental order.

Different grades of being exist even outside the mind. The lowest grade is something that is completely material; for example, a rock. The vegetable realm, which has some kind of activity, obviously possesses more being, more reality, more perfection than the rock, since it is capable of nutrition, growth and reproduction. An animal belongs to a grade of reality higher than the rock because it can nourish itself, like the vegetable; but it is also superior to the latter, for it enjoys the possession of sense life. Sense life is also possessed by the soul of man, but the soul has in addition the powers of choice and intellection. The soul is not less real, less solid than a rock. Its reality is more full, more dense, more complete, more satisfying than the reality of the rock because it is capable of higher activities. Man leads a more interesting life than a rock; his activities are more varied because he is capable of thought and decision.

Sanctifying grace is on the next higher step in this extra-mental order. It is an extra-mental reality—not the content of a thought, of a decision or of an affection. It exists in the soul, but it does not exist there as the content of a thought or of a decision. It is not something nebulous but is something more real and complete in existence, in being, in perfection than the soul itself. Grace acts as a new vital principle, a fundamental principle of activity and life, giving specific perfections. Man can act in a specifically different manner when he possesses it. This new activity is knowing and loving as God knows and loves Himself, activities which properly belong to the nature of God.

Catholic theology stresses this fact because Lutherans maintain that when man is converted, he grasps the merits of Christ by his faithful trust, is converted and changed in his way of thinking, deciding and loving. It is true that man does change his way of thinking, of loving—and in fact the whole direction of his life—but he changes because a new physical reality has been implanted in him which enables him to do so. Man is not merely changed or altered in his ethical or moral relationships to God, he is changed in the order of being itself. It is important to appreciate the value of being itself if we wish to understand what sanctifying grace really is.

This distinction is vital. Two acts identical in the moral order can be distinguished in terms of the power by which each is done: one may arise from grace and the other not; one, therefore, may be valuable for heaven and the other not. This power in the soul whereby the Christian lives the life of grace is therefore a physical reality.

Let us suppose that a savage has been baptized through desire. Believing that God exists, rewards and punishes, believing that God has revealed this, he accepts it on His word, desiring to do everything that God wants him to do. In his tribe, however, certain customs are infractions of one or other of the commandments of God as we know them. The man believes that these customs are in accordance with God's will—in other words, he believes that what is in fact an objectively bad act is good. He and the Christian live lives which are morally in contradiction to one another; yet the savage at his final judgment could well be accounted the better man. Although the content of his *moral* activity was quite different, he may have used the grace given him to his fullest capacity. So there is much importance to be allocated to the physical as an element of grace.

Grace, then, is a physical gift; it is also a permanent one. It continues to exist in the soul, not as a series of transient aids given to man but as something like a new soul—a permanent, durable principle of activity. Unless one commits a mortal sin, it will remain as the root of all supernatural activities. The existentialists describe grace as a dialogue with God, but underlying this dialogue with God there is an ontological reality which gives it foundation—namely, the created reality of sanctifying grace.

An Intrinsic Change

The process of justification is that divine action by which God makes man just, rightly disposed towards God, in being and in action. In justification sins, original and personal, are truly deleted. The individual acts are obviously not taken away; one cannot take away something that has happened. But guilt is truly deleted. This is in opposition to the Lutheran position that sin is not annihilated but covered over. In addition man is internally renewed, is intrinsically changed. The Catholic teaching on justification continues the thread of God's revelation in the Old Testament.

In St. Paul (whom the Protestants wrongly claim as their advocate), justification means that man is constituted just, internally changed, made just before God. Obviously, then, man is not still a sinner, for the two concepts are not compatible. St. Paul stresses clearly in Romans 5:19 that Adam's fault constituted man internally a sinner and that Christ constitutes man internally just. St. Paul uses the phrase "washes away"; the process of washing is not the process of covering up or over. There are other such expressions in the New Testament. St. John, for example, says that Christ came to "take away sin." To take something away is not to leave it in place and cover it over. In Luke 10:34 we read that the wounds of the man were healed. The process of healing a wound is not simply to paint it over so that it is not seen, but to change it internally. St. Paul and St. John speak of baptism or of justification as a rebirth. At birth one is given the nature of the one from whom he is born; if one is born of human parents, he will be human. And if, as St. John repeats, man is born of God, it is expected that he will be divinized; that he will have a new nature or principle of life. A new life is something real, something positive, something intrinsic to man which develops as he develops. The activity of another cannot develop one's own life; only something intrinsic can do that.

A Share in God's Nature

Man is made a sharer in the divine nature and an adopted son of God. By this is meant that man has some kind of real participation in the nature of God. Man does not become united to God in a pantheistic fashion, as though he were another God. Nor is he united to God substantially as the humanity of Christ was united to God, so that we might say of any Christian: he is God. He remains a distinct personality and a nature diverse from God. And he is united to Him in a union which can be lost; Christ could not lose the hypostatic union. Man's union with God is an accidental one because grace, the bond between them, is an accident. The union, however, is real, it is not only in the order of thought and affection and will, as is one which binds a friend to a friend. This kind of union does indeed exist between the Christian and God, but another more real union exists, as we have said, in the extramental order. Grace is a share in the nature of God.

The nature of God is such that His characteristic activities are the spiritual activities of knowing and loving Himself, and it is a share in God's nature as a principle of operation which man is given when he receives the supernatural life of grace. By it he is enabled to act in somewhat the same way that God Himself acts. He is given in embryo, as it were, in the present life what he will receive in its fullness in heaven—the power to see God as He sees Himself, face-to-face, intuitively, without the intermediation of any idea. This is not natural to man. Without grace man is able to know God only through ideas: through grace he begins to know God as He is, though in obscurity. But this capacity for seeing God is, as we have said, in embryo; it cannot be actuated until man has passed through the condition of death.

Man is also made an adopted son of God. Adoption is defined as the taking of a stranger into a household. Someone who is not a member of the family, who has not been physically generated by the father, is adopted as son and heir, so that he will share in the family goods. Unlike human adoption, divine adoption is not founded on loneliness or need on God's part. Moreover, the divine adoption proceeds in a different fashion from human adoption. When man adopts, he takes one of the same nature as himself. God, however, does not find man possessing a nature similar to His own but constructs this similarity of nature in man through the gift of grace. When a human son is adopted he generally receives the inheritance of the father only at the father's death. Man receives the divine inheritance immediately, for grace is the seed of glory. The divine goods are given to man at the moment he is adopted, at baptism. Unlike human adoption, divine adoption changes man intrinsically. It is not purely a juridical fiction, but lies midway between an act of genuine generation and a legal fiction. It has some of the characteristics of each, because man receives a real similarity of nature, such as usually occurs by generation; but though he is deified, he does not become God.

This, then, is the internal renovation that occurs at justification: one is made a sharer in the nature of God, becomes a child of God. The just man is born of God, he is His son. If the new nature is a share in God's nature, then man has had his sins removed. The scriptural proofs for the whole process of justification can be anchored to the notion of generation. If man is generated by God, from having been an enemy, he becomes a son. If man is a son he is genuinely loved by the Father, and hence he cannot be a sinner. If he is a son, then he is internally renewed and changed for the better. As St. John says: "the seed of God remains permanently within the justified man." Generation results in the communication of nature—a radical, fundamental principle of activity. Because he shares in the life of the Head, Christ, man should manifest the kind of decisions characteristic of Him, the ethical life characteristic of Him, for the wild grape grafted onto the vine produces sweet fruit.

6

GRACE AND
JUSTIFICATION

FUNDAMENTAL to the entire Christian idea of grace is the Pauline idea of justification. Since this notion has been subject to misunderstanding on the part of some non-Catholics, discussion of it is necessary. We should recall first that Paul is a Jew, with an Old Testament background, so that when he is speaking of the justice of God and God's justifying action on the human soul he is frequently doing so against this Old Testament background. The root concept of the "justice of God" we find in Romans 3:21-26: "But now the justice of God has been made manifest independently of the Law, being attested by the Law and the Prophets; the justice of God through faith in Jesus Christ upon all who believe. For there is no distinction, as all have sinned and have need of the glory of God. They are justified freely by his grace through the redemption which is in Christ Jesus, whom God has set forth as a propitiation by his blood through faith, to manifest his justice, God in his patience remitting former sins; to manifest his justice at the present time, so that he himself is just, and makes just him who has faith in Jesus." And again: "For, ignorant of the justice of God and seeking to establish their own, they have not submitted to the justice of God" (Rom. 10:3). These statements are profoundly influenced by the climate of the Old Testament.

Few scholars seem to agree on precisely how to approach the problem of the justice of God in the Old Testament. Some treat justice as a concept with a history, as an institution that evolved from earliest times to the prophets. According to them the modifications undergone by the concept changed it essentially, and these changes can be shown in their various stages. Others attempt to prove that the administration of divine justice admits of no contradictions in the sense that God is more consistent than can be fathomed. Still others deal mainly with the notion of justice or justness as a divine principle, as it were, preserving the consistency of divine dealings with men. Finally, there are some who suggest that the administration of divine justice always involved suffering as just punishment for violation of the moral code.

The differences of approach among these authors force the adoption of an artificial outline of their thinking in order to consider and evaluate the points on which they agree or disagree. As a result, the justice of God will be treated according to three concepts: the notion of justice, justice as a divine attribute, and justice and its administrations. Each of these will then be studied according to three aspects: basis, characteristics and aims, implications.

The Notion of Justice

The Hebrew term *sedeqah,* which is rendered as justice or righteousness in English and as *justice* in French, is usually taken to mean conformity to a norm. *Sedeq* denotes what is right, stable and substantial. In its widest sense, righteousness was virtually synonymous with propriety. But in the Old Testament, righteousness, even in this sense, has a more limited significance. While the fundamental idea of *sedeq* available to us is the state corresponding to a norm, which remains to be defined in each particular case, and while righteousness has the general meaning of fidelity to a state or a way of acting or thinking, justice is by no means a static concept. For it is the result of righteousness, and righteousness is a dynamic conception. Righteousness, then, is used not only to designate the *state of justice* but also that which produces it.

But the norms according to which a state of being may be considered righteous must be examined. For not only is justice not static, it is also not abstract. The norms of justice are those which prevail between man and man; as such they are concrete; the *right standards* of a nation or of a society. In its ultimate social significance, justice is that proper relation between men which is brought about by the exercise of justice. For one man to offend another is to create an injustice because violence has been done to the proper relation between them. But they are restored to a just state whenever justice is exercised on behalf of the man offended. Now conformity to a rule, of course, varies according to the subjects who produce it; but in contacts between men and men or between God and men, righteousness is always a concept of relationship, fashioned upon the everyday dealings between two people and varying according to the requirements arising from their contacts.[1]

In determining whether a state of affairs is just or unjust, a higher authority must render a judgment; so it may be said that justice as an active force is most clearly defined when it is associated with the activity of a judge. When justice is attributed to God, it is always considered in relation to His judicial activity. It is the judgment of God, moreover, which sets the norms for justice and maintains just situations. Justice or righteousness to the Hebrew may then be equated with rectitude, denoting both the state of affairs and that which produces and maintains it. It is, in sum, a judicial, moral and ethico-religious concept, which in its applications to God takes on unique significance.

Justice a Divine Attribute

It was natural for the Jews to regard Jahweh as a God of justice. In the first place Jahweh was looked upon almost as a chief of the

Hebrews. Since it was one of the functions of a Semitic tribal chieftain to judge and to uphold the "right" state of affairs in the community, the Jews easily saw Jahweh's role as that of judge. That this attitude toward the divinity was not uncommon among the Semites may be seen in the Babylonian worship of Ba'al as supreme judge over his people. Indeed, the primary attribute of moral perfection is righteousness—that is, the moral exactitude with which God applies His own perfect standard without fear, partiality, or selfishness, whenever His revelation finds expression.

In the Old Testament God is indeed righteous, but His righteousness is always associated with power. He is righteous in His judgments, and He judges because He is powerful. Furthermore, the judgments of Jahweh always conform to the rule; being right they attain their end, which is the establishment of His kingship. There is a purpose to God's justice always; it is to re-establish the right as He sees it. But precisely what God's aim is and how he accomplishes it in each case are matters demanding careful examination.[2]

We have already seen that Jahweh's justice is attributed to Him first in His role as head of the Jewish people. He is the all-powerful king whose will is done, whose will establishes the right. But God's will is a holy one, it accomplishes the requirements of the *moral* order. Indeed, God demonstrates His holiness by acting righteously. Holiness, then, is another basis for the divine justice. To be holy, in the moral order, is to be "right," and it is the moral order that most concerned the Jews. Indeed, the Hebrew conception of deity could not but include the notion of righteousness. Finally, divine power is also a basis for Jahweh's justice as a personal attribute.

But divine justice had a peculiar significance for the Jews; it had a historical basis in the covenant made between God and Moses that associated Jahweh with one of the Semite tribes. To Moses and to his people, God promised deliverance in return for which He demanded obedience to His law. From this point the Jewish understanding of deliverance determines the precise significance of divine justice.

In the first place the Hebrew notion of history was dominated by the idea of just divine retribution for sin. The plight of man was considered the direct and just result of the original sin of Adam. That God responds *justly* to the activities of men was always implicit in the Jewish conception of divinity. With the merciful He is merciful; with the perfect, perfect; with the pure, pure; that is, He is the living standard of moral order. As Lord of Creation, Jahweh is first concerned with establishing justice in every sphere, and especially in the moral order. He is, therefore, the judge of *all* men. The first historical basis for attributing justice to God, then, is the fact that the universe is His creation and, as a just God, He will not tolerate injustice in any people. For this reason the divine governance of the world as a whole was deemed a just one by the Jews. God in His government always does what is suitable, that is, whatever fulfills His aim.

Justice was further associated with the faithfulness of God. However, this did not mean that God was bound to observe the same faithfulness in His dealings with all men. The judgment of Jahweh is always made with *sedeqah*—that is, according to His sovereignty, which is the norm; and though the norm is often exercised within a judicial framework, it can also shatter it, since the institutions of the law depend on Jahweh's own freedom. God, then, was not bound by law, but had an ethical freedom which allowed Him to enter into legal contracts with only a portion of the human race. And in being faithful to His contract, God was making manifest His justice. Or, to put it another way, God, by being just, was also being faithful to His contract. He betrothed Himself to the Jewish people, and justice was to be the hallmark of the agreement. If the contract was violated, the agreement would remain in force, but God would be free to right the wrong. Although God had a claim on the obedience of every Jew, every Jew had a special claim on the justice of God, a right to expect that a just state of affairs would prevail in the world as a result of their mutual agreement.

We recall that the state of affairs wherein justice is most appropriately operative is the relationship between men and men, and men and God. Where men offended other men, injustice was done, and this demanded correction. It was presumed that the offended man or men were just, and that the offender was unjust. The offended party could then appeal to God for restoration of whatever was lost. As the notion of a just state of affairs developed in Israel, the restoration demanded by an offended party took on a new character. Whereas formerly restoration of justice had meant simple compensation for the wrong done the man or the nation, it now began to mean something more. For implicit in the divine promise of deliverance was the condition that the men of Israel be morally upright, as part of the agreement and for their own salvation. Thus when an individual or a nation offended God, the offense was met with a response that re-established the proper state of affairs. But that proper state of affairs was not simply a judicial matter, but related to the promised deliverance. Hence God's judgment on some one man or nation (the exercise of His justice) had the aim of restoring the wicked man or people to favor in the eyes of God in order that their salvation might be effected. Thus the sinner also had a claim of sorts on divine justice, for once restoration was made he too became upright and was declared righteous once more. But the conditions of his restoration and the change in Jewish thought which led to the notion must await further examination before any conclusions can be drawn.

It may be said, then, that insofar as justice is an attribute of God, it has three features. It is attributed to the holy God who commits no iniquity, who cannot leave wickedness unpunished or the good unrecognized, who is merciful and slow to anger, desiring not the death of the sinner but that he should repent and live. It is attributed to the God of love who pursues the salvation of His people;

and finally it is attributed to the God of love who communicates His righteousness to the sinner and justifies him.[3]

History of the Concept

Scholars do not question that there is a difference between the early and the final Hebrew attitude towards divine justice as presented in the Old Testament. In pre-Exilic times retribution is seen as the ultimate objective of God in correcting injustice, and in the post-Exilic times the divine motive is perhaps love. Where the authorities disagree is in their explanation of the difference.

The Jews always believed that God rewards the good and punishes the evil. Adam and Eve were banished from the Garden of Eden, and the lot of all mankind is a result of the Fall, a perpetual punishment for the primal disobedience. Only Noe and his family were saved in the flood. The cities of Sodom and Gomorrha perished in flames as a result of their iniquity, and only Lot, the one just man living in the area, was saved.

It is important to note that the first characteristic of the judgment of God is that it extends to all men; all are subject to the divine will. Jahweh is not solely the God of Israel, He is ruler of humanity; He determines international morality. And here we have an illustration of the freedom attributed to God even in the earliest Jewish thought. For God has delivered other nations as well as Israel. God guarantees the moral order of all nations.

At the time of the first biblical writers, justice was seen as retributive; penalty was imposed for a crime, and this was always in the temporal order. God's punishment is immediate and extends not only to the sinner but to all those associated with him, whether by family or nation. Thus the covenant given to Moses implied the degree of moral solidarity expected of the Jews by God. Guilt extends to a man's descendants. Joab's descendants, for example, would suffer because he was a murderer. People suffer for the mistakes of their leaders; justice is, in other words, collective and is intended to compensate for the wrong that induces its administration.[4]

Atonement for sin was possible, however, in the elaborate purification rites prescribed in Exodus. Justice demanded that the guilty suffer for their sin, or the sin of one of their number, but when the punishment had been imposed, there was always opportunity for justification of the guilty. Furthermore, sin is always considered to be disobedience. Adam disobeyed the command of God when he sinned. In essence, sin for the Jew was rebellion against superior authority, which demanded punishment. Even in the time of the prophets sin is considered to be rebellion against God.

Rebellion for the Jews, of course, took the form of disobedience to the commandments of God. When the sin of a Jew was great enough to merit chastisement of a high order, all Israel suffered, generally at the hands of other nations or from natural disasters. The blessings conferred on Israel at the making of the covenant were withdrawn, and the result was shortening of life, childlessness, scarcity and famine, in order that Israel might know that it possessed all natural blessings only as a gift of God. Such penalties are always considered the result of just divine judgments. And although the punishment is always suited to the crime, God's judgment is never so severe as to allow it to be fully in accordance with the gravity of the sin committed. His mercy is always shown in one fashion or other, there is always a call to repentance and with it the possibility of repentance, and there is always a remnant that is saved. And indeed the people are always given an opportunity to repent of their error before they are punished. Repentance may not forestall punishment, but whenever the sinner repents before his punishment, he is subjecting himself to the judgment of God in the best possible manner. Justice is always seen as aimed at restoring Israel to God. It has a purpose; for if condign satisfaction were demanded for sin, death would be the only acceptable punishment.

Finally, in His seemingly preferential treatment of Israel, God was not being unjust. As we have observed, He has an ethical freedom which permitted justifiable contract-making. It may be said, in addition, that God's judgment of other nations was in accord with His justice at all times.[5]

Some suggest that it was Ezechiel who first proposed that justice had meaning for the individual, and that each man suffered for his own sins, although still in the temporal order. The *jus talionis* remained the basis for judgment. Still the theocracy of Israel was considered to be temporal, with blessing and punishment to be dispensed on earth. Man's lot, we recall, is the result of his moral state. The good man should prosper, the evil man suffer. That the Jews expected this to be the case is evident in the Book of Job, where the sufferings of Job seem to have no cause, and he asks why the evil prosper and the good suffer. When, on occasions, God did show patience with the wicked, we may say that it was for some higher purpose.

Justice Applied to Individual Man

With the prophets is introduced the notion that justice and justification do not have their primitive significance. The divine response to sin and to the appeal of the wronged man has a new purpose. The aim of justice is to restore individual men to their proper relation with God in order that they may be better men who will perhaps receive reward after death. In earlier Jewish thought, the afterlife was virtually the same in character for the just and the unjust. Now it was to assume new importance. Now the aim of justice is not simply to re-establish an abstract moral order; it is to justify every man on an absolute scale. Suffering for sin is no longer the primary feature of justification. The individual just man can now claim the justice of God. At the end of his life the soul of the just man will return to the Lord. The psalmists preach a final transformation of the just. Hades will become a place of punishment for the unjust. Finally a sort of resurrection of the just is implied in the apocalyptic writers.[6]

The chief feature of justice and its primary objective was the pardoning of sins. Moreover, the justice of God found perfect compatibility with His goodness and mercy. But God could not do more than chastise, He could not restore an uncoöperative man. The Jews realized that justification in its ultimate sense was a two-sided process. Only the just man could receive divine favor; even the most heartfelt prayers of the *unjust* man were of no avail. In its final sense the justice of God amounted to love of the sinner and hatred for his sin.[7]

This was not merely an exterior justice, although it was a judiciary justice, for it ensured that God Himself at the end of time would proclaim this man just at His tribunal. However, this declaratory act of God recognized an objective justice which the Jew had antecedently possessed because of his observance of the law, the integral and adequate expression of God's will. Though the Jew had observed the law and was interiorly just, this justice was not final until it had been recognized by God on the day of judgment. God's act of justifying man in the Old Testament was not an act which rendered an unjust man just. It was an act which recognized in a judicial form the justice which the Jew had already acquired by faithful observance of the law.[8]

Some authorities maintain that this judiciary notion of justification is not to be found through all the Old Testament, and they make particular exception of the prophets. It is, however, a frequent notion in Old Testament thought, and it carries with it the characteristic idea that justice is in its essence eschatological. Final recognition, divine recognition and proclamation of man's justice will take place only on the day of judgment. When this day arrives God will publicly proclaim man just and by this sentence will grant him title to enter into the messianic kingdom, to share in the messianic goods. The right which God concedes at this final moment is the right to the hereditary good of the Messiah; it is a decree that the just Jew may be admitted into eternal life. This is the general outline of the notion of justification as an act on God's part as it is found in the Old Testament. It is important to keep it in mind, since St. Paul will frequently use some of these ideas, modifying and transforming them for his own particular purpose.

Justice in St. Paul

This Old Testament declarative or legal sense of justice can certainly be found in St. Paul. It is perhaps more frequent in the Epistle to the Romans than elsewhere, but it is not the exclusive Pauline meaning of justification. The eschatological concept of justice is also attached by St. Paul to justification, for God's decree grants access to eternal life, as we read in Galatians 3:11: "But that by the law no man is justified before God is evident, because 'he who is just lives by faith' "; or in Galatians 3:21: "Is the law then contrary to the promises of God? By no means"; or in Titus 3:7: "in order that, justified by his grace, we may be heirs of life everlasting."

While St. Paul frequently uses justification in this sense it is not always presented as a future good to be obtained at the last moment, but often refers to the present, as in 1 Corinthians 6:11: "And such were some of you, but you have been washed, you have been sanctified, you have been justified in the name of our Lord Jesus Christ, and in the Spirit of our God." The fact of the matter is that St. Paul has profoundly transformed the notion of justification which he drew from the Old Testament. For St. Paul, as for the entire primitive Christian community, the eschatological times are already present, the last times of the Church are now.[9]

Paul's is a realized eschatology. Christ has risen from the dead not only as the head of the column of humanity but as one who incorporates all of us into Him. Hence, Christ by His resurrection has anticipated the last times. Those Christians who have been baptized into the Christ have also died to themselves and risen to Him, to new life in Him, and live in the last times. They are members of the Christ and consequently they form with Him one mystical unity. So Pauline justification, even when it points to the eschatological times, is by no means the Jewish way of looking towards the end of time. For the Christian the end of time has already radically arrived with the resurrection of Christ. The Pauline notion of justification, while it looks to the future, looks to a future already present in germ. The Christian, having already risen, is to seek the things that are above; his conversation should be in heaven because he is in the last times now. The old things have passed away and the new man has been created. "Therefore you are now no longer strangers and foreigners, but you are citizens with the saints and members of God's household" (Ephes. 2:19). "He has rescued us from the power of darkness and transferred us into the kingdom of his beloved Son, in whom we have our redemption, the remission of our sins" (Col. 1:13).

What is completely fresh and unique in Pauline theology is this notion that the messianic goods do not have to be waited for but are already communicated to the Christian.

Paul also modifies the Old Testament notion of justification in another fashion. To the Jew justification was gained through the observance of the law. It was the individual Jew who personally gave to himself his justice, obtained it by his own proper powers, by observing the law—which, of course, was itself a grace from God, since by it God indicated to the Jew how he was to please Him. By observing the law the Jew entered into a sort of juridical contract with God so that his own personal work could render him just.[10]

The Judaizers

This approach to justification was what gave St. Paul so much trouble in the primitive Christian community, for those whom we call the Judaizers insisted upon the observation of the law to justify man. In the Epistle to the Galatians, St. Paul strongly censures this group, pointing out that the Christian concept of justification is quite different from theirs. The Pauline concept of justification is that God declares us just and thereby effectively makes us so. Pauline justification is not merely declarative; on the contrary, it is constitutive. This characteristic distinguishes it completely from Jewish theology, since in that theology it was not God who justified man but man who justified himself through the works of the law, graciously given to him by God. Paul insists that we are free from the law, and yet we are justified, not through practice of the law but through the grace of God. The Judaizing Christians granted a certain role to Christ, the role of Exemplar and of Saviour in the sense that Christ constituted a great treasury of merits for them, as Abraham and the prophets had done. To Paul, Christ is much more than that, He is the Saviour who has established an entirely new economy. The observance of the law is no longer necessary; in fact, it has become impossible. The law can no longer give justice to man, yet man is just because God freely acts to justify and constitute man holy. Man is just because God communicates, by a gratuitous act of love, a share in His own divine life to him. Impotent as man is to justify himself, he will nevertheless be justified in the Christian economy through the activity of Another who will transform man's inmost being. The instrument of this justification, this shared holiness, is the Christ—His life, His death and above all His paschal mystery. Our justice is Christ, and the justice of Christ is the justice of God in which we share. As Paul says in 2 Corinthians 5:21: "For our sakes he made him to be sin who knew nothing of sin, so that in him we might become the justice of God."[11]

Imputed Justice

Protestant theologians frequently admit that in some sense we are rendered just through Christ our Saviour, but they usually insist that this justice is not constitutive of any new inner state on our part. Rather, they say, God permits Christ to take our place, and although we remain sinners, God does not view us as such, for He looks upon us in Christ. In other words, the justice of Christ is not interior to us, but is imputed to us; we remain sinners, but God does not see our sins because He looks upon us in Christ whom He has constituted our justice.

In contrast to this Protestant concept of justification St. Paul states clearly that our justice is not imputed and external but is interior and immanent. It does not suffice to believe that Christ's justice reconciles us with God. Rather His death is the cause of our interior penetration by the Spirit of Christ, the Holy Spirit, who is poured into our souls.

We cannot reduce the Pauline mysticism of the mystical body to any kind of an exterior imputation of holiness. Christ communicates His Spirit to us, unites us to Himself and causes our whole ethical conscience and our whole ontological being to be transformed so that we think the thoughts of Christ, choose the choices of Christ and live by His being. The Spirit of Christ causes a holy ordination of our will which justifies us interiorly and transforms our very being.

Protestant theologians generally pay little attention to the concept of this interior Spirit given us in justification. At times they do say that the Spirit is communicated to us in an interior fashion and that He produces in us the good works of sanctification, but in their understanding these good works properly speaking belong to the Spirit: they testify to His presence in man but do not properly belong to man. According to Pauline theology, the Spirit enters into us and changes our hearts, sanctifies us by separating us from all that is profane and makes us conformed to God Himself. The Spirit elevates us to the sacred order and gives us the power to conquer sin. We are thus placed in an entirely new position, in a normal relationship to God, by justification. The works of the Spirit are not, as it were, external to us; they are our proper works done in the power which He grants to us.

The great Protestant theologian Karl Barth insists that our justice is not ours but remains extrinsic to us. He resists the idea of an interior sanctification because he conceives it as a juridical right by which we would make fructify and develop a small treasure of grace which is given to us. We understand his insight, which is a primitive Christian one—namely, that the justice communicated to the Christian always remains the justice of God even when communicated. It is never a separate entity, but is a being directed towards union with God. It cannot be conceived separately from the justice of God or the justice of Christ, but remains the justice of Christ, although genuinely interior and operative *within us.* It points always to its source, Christ. We remain always dependent upon God in our works even when we merit, for the principle of merit is itself a grace.

It is true that at times theologians speak in a way scarcely conformed to this Pauline theology, but in authentic Christian thought grace remains a gift from God as long as we possess it. The Catholic does not wish to imply that grace emanates from the natural soul. What is communicated to us is truly ours, but it also remains the justice of Christ. We do not create our own justice; it is within us, but it is always within as a gift.

Our justice is truly ours, and yet it remains imperfect. The Protestants insist that the imperfections which remain in us even after justification are such as to eliminate any possibility of merit. Reiterating that grace is not a stock which we can invest for eternal life, they place a radical cleavage between the world of promises here and our fulfillment in eternity. Paul, on the contrary, insists that grace is homogeneous with heaven. For St. Paul our new life is spiritual, not merely carnal, and this spirituality renders us capable of eternal life. We already live the life of the last times, the messianic goods are already communicated to us in germ, and we have only to make them fructify. Obviously, this fructification cannot take place without the work of God. The prime initiative is always given to God, and God always has the primacy of activity in our salvation.

A New Being

In St. Paul one finds not the doctrine of Luther but the doctrine of the Council of Trent, which declares that God's justice is interiorly communicated to us. St. Paul employs many different formulations to make us realize this. He says that we are given a share in the life of Christ risen from the dead, a participation which causes us to be mystically, although really, united with Christ without losing the boundaries of our own personality. He speaks of the Christian as a new being, a new creature filled with justice, sanctity and grace, enjoying the life of Christ and possessing the Spirit of Christ. All these aspects of justification—life, grace, holiness—have been isolated by the Protestants from the parallel Pauline doctrine, and they have thus impoverished the idea of justification, making it, as we have seen, an imputed thing. Instead, all the currents of the rich Pauline synthesis should be merged into a unity, since Paul is attempting by many expressions to show forth the essential nature of the change that is produced by grace. The Spirit communicates to us the life of Christ and sanctifies us. The life of the risen Christ is active in our life and constitutes us living by a new life. God the eternal Father grants His grace or His justice and concedes to men the redemption of Jesus Christ through the Holy Spirit. Justification grants to us a new nature, as it were, a supernature working a profound transformation of our natural being, elevating us into the divine order. The justice of God, divine salvation, is granted to us in His mercy, re-creating us as new beings.

Paul insists that justification is many-faceted, including the complete extinction of sin. Sin is not merely covered over by the merits of Christ but is completely removed. The law of the spirit of life in Christ Jesus has liberated me from the law of sin and death. At times when Paul speaks of the non-imputation of sins, of sin as remitted, covered, we can only deduce from the entire Pauline synthesis that these expressions are equivalent to "taken away." The Christian is renewed internally, as Ephesians 4:20-24 points out clearly: "But you have not so learned Christ—for surely you have heard of him and have been taught in him (as truth is in Jesus) that as regards your former manner of life you are to put off the old man, which is being corrupted through its deceptive lusts. But be renewed in the spirit of your mind, and put on the new man, which has been created according to God in justice and holiness of truth." We have put off the old man, and we are capable of being renewed in spirit, of taking on an entirely new life in the Spirit who is given to us in grace. We have put on the new man created after the image of God, justice and the sanctity of truth. It is baptism which gives us this new humanity, and it is baptism which makes us a new creature.

Faith and Justification

Luther, in his interpretation of the Epistle to the Romans, insisted that justice comes to us only through faith. In order to hold the doctrine that works are useless he rejected the entire Epistle of St. James. This aspect of Lutheran theology has brought confusion to many Christian minds, since it is undoubtedly true that Paul does ascribe our justification to faith. It would be well, therefore, to examine briefly the relationship between faith and justification in Pauline theology. Since Paul holds that our faith is what justifies us, we must realize that Pauline "faith" can be used in a plenary sense peculiar to him.

The Pauline conception of faith frequently means that powerful element of the Christian life which is not merely an assent to a theoretical truth but a rich and complex engagement of the entire man, will and intelligence. It is a commitment to the person of Christ which contains the homage of obedience to his laws, charity and love and knowledge of Christ. This type of faith is indeed justifying, because it is itself informed by charity, or grace.

Faith can be counted for justice in St. Paul if one takes faith in this plenary sense, which the apostle often gives it, a faith animated by charity. In Thomistic language one would say that this faith animated by charity is the last disposition to justification. It is the last disposition to the entrance of the form grace into the soul; but in Thomistic doctrine the last disposition is produced by the form itself, so that this plenary faith would be formed by charity, or grace itself. This type of faith is an instrumental cause, because human collaboration enters into it, a material cause because it is a disposition to grace, and a formal cause because plenary faith is indistinguishable from charity itself; it is justification considered in the process of becoming, from the viewpoint of becoming just.

However, faith which is not informed by charity is by no means justifying. It is simply a preparatory disposition required for justification but insufficient itself. It is merely one of the conditions required that a man become just.

Our justice is still gratuitous even when it depends upon our works, because the radical principle for all merit is itself the original gift of grace. While our justification implies activity on our part, still the only reason that we can act in the divine order is the original gift of grace; hence justification through the law and Christian justification are completely different. The works which we observe are not simply ours, as were the works of the Jews of the Old Testament, but remain gratuitous gifts, since their first principle, grace, comes from God. In the same way the activity of faith is indeed ours, but the power to produce it is given to us from above and requires the free operation of the Holy Spirit. All of our good works in the divine order are done with the collaboration of the Holy Spirit, who always has primacy over us. Hence justice and gratuity exist at the same time in the Christian dispensation. Our justice is at once ours and a gift from Another. Our faith is an operation of our personal intelligence and of the creative Spirit working in our hearts. The Holy Spirit who presides at the genesis of faith is also necessary throughout our life to maintain it and to assist us to produce the works of faith. We are not simply justified and left to our own devices, grace is not simply an independent entity which can bear fruit without the further assistance of God. We have indeed been renewed in the Spirit of Christ and entered into a new life, but we are always dependent upon this vivifying Spirit who has entered into us.

Most Protestants today admit that the Lutheran notion of justification is by no means that of early Christianity. They claim that the Fathers, especially the Greek Fathers, taught what is the doctrine of the present-day Roman Church. The Greek Fathers understood the mystical union of the Christian with Christ and his deification by the indwelling Spirit. According to the Protestants, this was a departure from Pauline theology produced through a mixture of oriental influences and non-Christian sources.

However, theological reflection should convince us that God's love is surely as efficacious as man's. God cannot declare a man just without rendering him just. It is true that in the past certain theologians, the predecessors of Luther, claimed that God could, by an absolute exercise of his power, declare a man just while he still remained sinful. But St. Thomas—along with subsequent Christian thought—rejected this position, and did so rightly. The will of God effects a change in man. When God loves He produces in the loved object its beauty. His effective love and His affective love are one. If God accepts man and looks upon him graciously, by this very act He produces an effect in man, the term. Otherwise we should have to suppose that God's subjective will is constantly changing, each time man changes from sinner to saint, which would be absurd.

Lutheran doctrine has insisted overmuch upon one aspect of Christian thought while detaching it from the complementary aspect which would give it its full truth.[12] According to Catholic doctrine all sins are totally taken away, although man is left not yet perfect but subject to an indeliberate, non-free inclination for sin when he has once been wounded by sin.

The Double Justification Theory

It is true that certain Catholic theologians before the time of Luther and the Council of Trent had spoken of justification in a way little conformed to Pauline theology. Some theologians of Cologne proposed a theory by which they hoped to reconcile the Lutheran with the Catholic position and establish religious peace. In the opinion of this school, of whom Seripando and Gropper were the most notable representatives, the Christian's justice would be constituted by a double perfection: first by a gratuitous gift of God internal to the soul which we call sanctifying grace. But this justification would be imperfect, requiring another justice, not inherent in us but external, imputed to us extrinsically, namely, the merits of Christ. Without this second, complementary, imputed justice we would not be formally justified. Thus, according to the school of Cologne, our imperfect and inherent justice would be insufficient to constitute us genuinely just at the tribunal of God. Rather, we would always have to depend upon the mercy of God and the proper justice of Christ at the divine tribunal.

The Council of Trent did not approve this theory but declared that the unique formal, intrinsic cause of our justice was sanctifiying grace. Moreover, it declared that the just Christian has merited eternal life and needs nothing further for admission into the kingdom of God. The double justice theory had its roots in certain statements of medieval mystics who appear to show a tendency to downgrade the interior justice of man and to insist too sharply upon the fact that we are useless and unprofitable servants and at the hour of death can trust only in the merits of Christ. The Council of Trent[13] states that the unique formal cause of justification is the justice of God, not that justice by which He Himself is just, but that justice by which we are just, by which we are not reputed to be just but are truly called and are just, a justice which each one of us receives internally. In objecting to the double justice theory of Cologne, Trent insisted that one must not speak of an "imperfect justice" if this expression is to signify that sin is not destroyed in the Christian. Nevertheless, while one cannot admit that sin remains in the Christian after justification, we are not forbidden to use the expression "imperfect justice" if this means that our justice is accompanied by a certain continued, non-free preference for evil, namely, concupiscence. Moreover, even the just man cannot avoid all venial sin without a special privilege. That egotism which afflicts man from the beginning and which sanctifying grace gives him the radical power to conquer has not been completely destroyed in the justified man; concupiscence remains. Hence there is need for the mystical death and the mystical baptism of the sacraments and a continued life of mortification.[14]

In conclusion, we may not say that there are two formal causes for Christian justification. We are made just, but not by that Lutheran external imputation of the justice of Christ which serves as a complement to our imperfect justice. The Council of Trent insists that our justice is immanent to us and that the extrinsic attribution of Christ's justice does not determine our ultimate salvation. Nevertheless it is quite obvious that the council admits that our justice is always a participated justice, a share in Christ's justice and depends upon Christ's activity. We remain just because Christ and His Spirit continue to exert their influence upon us. Our justice is an actual share in the holiness of Christ because we are members of Christ and mystically one with Him. God sees us as just, but we are not just if we are separated from the Christ. Hence one can say in a certain sense that the Christian does found his hope upon his own proper intrinsic justice, but this justice is in no sense a separated and autonomous entity; grace is an entity of union. We have trust in ourselves only insofar as we are inserted into the living vine, Christ; it is always He who adapts us to those filial attitudes which the Father approves. It is doubtless this that the medieval mystics meant, but they had not a sufficiently explicit formulation of the details of the doctrine of the Mystical Body. Doubtless, too, this is what certain ascetical writers mean when they use ambiguous expressions concerning our distrust of our own justice.

Paul was among the first to use the terms justified and justification, and to use them so frequently that the Church, in giving the name justification to the infusion of first grace into the soul of the sinner, has adopted his terminology. At the infusion of grace God repairs the destructive forces of sin, grants remission of sin and restores a capacity for divine vision; in a word, He justifies man by restoring him to the supernatural state. The Council of Trent summarizes the Pauline doctrine in saying that "the justification of the sinner is a translation from the state in which a man is born, a child of the first Adam, to a state of grace and of the adoption of sons of God. If any one denies that by the grace of our Lord Jesus Christ, which is conferred in baptism, the guilt of original sin is remitted or says that the whole of that which belongs to the essence of sin is not taken away, let him be anathema."[15] Furthermore, in the seventh chapter, sixth section of the Council of Trent, we read that "justification is not only a remission of sin but also sanctification and a renewal of the inward man." As Paul puts it, "you have been washed, you have been sanctified, you have been justified in the name of Our Lord Jesus Christ" (1 Cor. 6:11). Just as Adam's disobedience had truly constituted us intrinsically sinners, so "as by the disobedience of the one man the many were constituted sinners, so also by the obedience of the one (Christ) the many will be constituted just" (Rom. 5:19).

St. Thomas

The opinion of St. Thomas, which is the one most widely accepted in theology today, maintains that so close is the relationship between grace and the remission of sin that not even God by His omnipotence could make sin and grace co-exist in the same soul. Just as grace always involves forgiveness of sin, in the real order there is no forgiveness that does not proceed from grace. There is no remission of sin without the infusion of grace, for the Council of Trent teaches: "If anyone says that men are justified by the sole remission of sins to the exclusion of grace and charity, let him be anathema." Perhaps this is why the Church, in her prayers and ritual, so frequently interchanges the ideas of justification, remission of sin and infusion of grace. The infusion of grace is all that is required for justification and the remission of sin. It has an anteriority but not a temporal priority to the remission of sin. The two, infusion of grace and remission of sin, are simultaneous in the order of time, but in the order of causal priority the infusion of grace is prior, since it brings about the remission of sin.

The moment grace enters, the soul is revivified and all acquisitions of the past, all previous merits, are revivified insofar as they increase eternal glory. Once a man is rooted in grace and planted in Christ he tends to remain there, becoming progressively stronger in his growth towards his divine end. The inclination of his heart and the judgments of his intellect are submitted to the motions of the Indwelling Spirit, and he tends to follow God and to judge creatures according to their right proportionate value. Grace rectifies the direction of the will and sets up an impulse towards God, an orientation which sets the soul in motion towards its final end. Hence the soul is rectified or justified, and in order to yield to sin it would have to go against the inclination of the fortified will.

We should note that sanctifying grace, which we have been discussing thus far, does not by itself necessarily cure man's moral inability to observe the entire moral law. Habitual or sanctifying grace is a constant principle, healing the moral weaknesses of man, restoring health to the soul which possesses it, and yet that soul will still need further actual graces in order to conquer severe temptation. Sanctifying grace suffices habitually to sanctify man by wiping out the stain of sin and putting an end to the disastrous moral disorder which serious sin involves. It separates man from moral impurity and consecrates him to God. It is the seal of God upon the soul, pointing out that this soul is reserved unto Himself. It is the seed of glory, and the Christian who possesses it is radically a saint. His sanctity will blossom into full splendor after this life of struggle. He who yields to the impulses of the Holy Spirit who dwells within him and allows this Holy Spirit progressively to direct his activity and his choices will bring to perfect fruit this germ of holiness.

If man has the misfortune to lose sanctifying grace, then he requires to be justified anew by the gracious gift of God. When at the tribunal of the sacrament of penance or through perfect contrition he again receives sanctifying grace, all his past merits, insofar as they constitute a treasure for his heavenly glory, are revivified. It is probable also that all the grace which he once possessed is restored to him at the moment when he regains sanctifying grace; if not, it is only because the subjective dispositions with which he approached justification were imperfect.

It is interesting to note that St. John and the Greek Fathers do not discuss justification in exactly the same terms in which St. Paul discusses it. The temperaments of St. John the mystic and of the Greek Fathers were such that they preferred to dwell upon the gifts of God, such as divine adoption. For someone such as Paul or Augustine, recent converts who had experienced the power of evil in their lives, grace would appeal very strongly as a healing power. Augustine will discuss grace under this aspect of justification also because he had personal experience that his flesh still remained rebellious. Graciously God used Augustine and Paul to lead us to a deeper understanding of the healing virtue and the justifying power of the mystery of grace.

NOTES

1. Jacob, *Theology of the Old Testament*, p. 94.

2. A. Descamps, "Justice," *Dictionnaire de la Bible, Supplément*, col. 1448.

3. H. Cazelles, "A propos de quelques difficultés relatifs à la justice de Dieu," *Revue Biblique* (1951), pp. 169 ff.

4. Heinisch, *Theology of the Old Testament*, p. 87.

5. Vriezen, *An Outline of Old Testament Theology*, p. 275.

6. A. Gelin, *The Key Concepts of the Old Testament* (New York, Sheed and Ward, 1955), p. 75. Cf. Eichrodt, *op. cit.*, pp. 114-120.

7. G. Kittel, ed., *Bible Key Words* (New York, Harper, 1951); see "Righteousness," by G. Quell and G. Schrenk, p. 5.

8. Guillet, *Themes of the Bible*, pp. 60 ff. Cf. E. Tobac, "Grace," *D.A.F.C.*, col. 325.

9. Tobac, art. cit., col. 326. Cf. Quell, art. cit., pp. 40-48.

10. Guillet, *op. cit.*, p. 87.

11. L. Cerfaux, "Justice," *Dictionnaire de la Bible, Supplément*, col. 1493.

12. J. Rivière, "Justification," *Dictionnaire de Théologie Catholique*, cols. 2150-2151.

13. Denzinger 799.

14. H. Jedin, *Papal Legate at the Council of Trent, Cardinal Seripando* (St. Louis, Herder, 1947), p. 359.

15. Denzinger 799 and 792 respectively.

7

GRACE AND FILIAL
ADOPTION

As WE HAVE SEEN in an earlier chapter, in the Old Testament God
acts to constitute the nation in the elected and permanent state of
sonship. This is an objective gift granted by Jahweh to His people,
and it establishes them in a situation which cannot be altered or
destroyed even if the individual member of the race proves unworthy, by his actions, of the divinely conferred prerogative. There
is no explicit understanding, in the Old Testament, of a transfigura-
tion of the individual's personality upon receipt of this privilege,
which comes to him by virtue of his physical descent from Abraham
or appurtenance to God's people. Sonship is seen clearly as one
more divine favor, similar to the covenant, the law, the institutional
and prophetic guidance God offered His people. The subject bene-
fiting by the divine action may remain interiorly untransformed,
with his personal status and relationship to God unchanged. The
sinner, Israel, is truly God's son when he defects from the supreme
moral will of Jahweh as well as when he obeys. Often Israel falls
far short of the divine demands, but its sonship is an inalienable
divine prerogative, an objective privilege independent of Israel's
justice, although soliciting the nation along the paths of righteousness.[1]

Later, St. Paul will grieve that many in the nation failed to conform their inner dispositions to the high dignity of election as sons
that God had conferred upon them: "I speak the truth in Christ, I

do not lie, my conscience bearing me witness in the Holy Spirit, that I have great sadness and continuous sorrow in my heart. For I could wish to be anathema myself from Christ for the sake of my brethren, who are my kinsmen according to the flesh; who are Israelites, who have the adoption as sons, and the glory and the covenants and the legislation and the worship and the promises; who have the fathers, and from whom is the Christ according to the flesh, who is, over all things, God blessed forever, amen" (Rom. 9:1-5).[2]

Some of the Jews did indeed live as befitted sons of God and were internally transformed by the grace of Christ, becoming true sons of Abraham, fitting sons of God: "Know therefore that the men of faith are the real sons of Abraham. And the Scripture, fore-seeing that God would justify the Gentiles by faith, announced to Abraham beforehand, 'In thee shall all the nations be blessed.' Therefore the men of faith shall be blessed with faithful Abraham" (Gal. 3:7-9). But in the days of later Judaism, these were perhaps the minority. Still the election and the status conferred placed Israel in a specific and unique relationship to God and independently of Israel's merits ensured that this nation would be the scene for God's providential actions in history.

Because of his membership in the race the individual Israelite may call upon God's mercy with confidence and expect the divine assistance to live as befits a son, even though, as we have seen, it is only relatively late in Old Testament times that the individual Jew addresses God as his father. But from the beginning he has easy access to the Most High and may address Him directly and with confidence. He is invited by Jahweh to internalize his ex-trinsic and objective prerogative and become truly an adopted son, a member of the internal and faithful Israel. Otherwise he will not belong in heart to the race of Abraham and his sonship will remain without an interior transforming power. "And whoever follow this rule, peace and mercy upon them even upon the Israel of God" (Gal. 6:16).

Israel God's Inheritance

From the beginning, God's election of Israel as His son is ordained towards the inner transformation of this people and for their interior sanctification. Israel is to be His inheritance as He is theirs, and His providence is assured to them. "Therefore, if you hearken to my voice and keep my covenant, you shall be my special possession, dearer to me than all other people, though all the earth is mine. You shall be to me a kingdom of priests, a holy nation" (Exod. 19:5-6).

The basis for God's choice is not the pre-existent merits of Israel but His limitlessly free love for him: "It was because the Lord loved you and because of his fidelity to the oath he had sworn to your fathers, that he brought you out with his strong hand from the place of slavery, and ransomed you from the hand of Pharaoh, king of Egypt. Understand, then, that the Lord, your God, is God indeed, the faithful God who keeps his merciful covenant down to the thousandth generation toward those who love him and keep his commandments, but who repays with destruction the person who hates him; he does not dally with such a one, but makes him personally pay for it" (Deut. 7:9,10).[3]

God warns Pharaoh that this love will not stand for interference, and if Pharaoh persists in his persecutions Jahweh will strike him. "So you shall say to Pharaoh; Thus says the Lord: Israel is my son, my first-born. Hence I tell you: Let my son go, that he may serve me. If you refuse to let him go, I warn you, I will kill your son, your first-born" (Exod. 4:22-23).

Between Jahweh and the people as a whole there is set up a relationship of love that Osee will later compare to the marriage relationship. Jahweh is a living and educating father and is capable of severity when Israel resists Him, but His punishments are always orientated towards Israel's salvation. At times Jahweh complains of the unfilial attitude of the people He has constituted His son: "Hear, O ye heavens, and give ear, O earth, for the Lord hath spoken. I have brought up children and exalted them: but they have despised me. The ox knoweth his owner and the ass his master's crib: but Israel hath not known me and my people hath not understood. Woe to the sinful nation, a people laden with iniquity, a wicked seed, ungracious children: they have forsaken the Lord, they have blasphemed the Holy One of Israel, they are gone away backwards" (Isa. 1:2-4).

"For my foolish people have not known me: they are foolish and senseless children. They are wise to do evil, but to do good they have no knowledge" (Jer. 4:22). "But as a woman that despiseth her lover, so hath the house of Israel despised me, saith the Lord" (Jer. 3:20).

Christ's Grace by Anticipation

The effect of this sonship in the interior of each individual is not necessarily any sharing in the divine nature, nor was it visualized as such by the Jews—far from it. But to those who are faithful to God, the transforming grace of Christ is given through the power of His cross. Israelite thought, even when it accented the individual's sharing in the nation's sonship, was not conscious of this internal transformation. The books, not part of the Jewish canon, which bear witness to the solicitude of Jahweh for the individual just man— His son—do not ascribe sonship to any internal participation in the nature of God. But the grace of Christ is present by anticipation in the just of the Old Testament and confers upon them a true internal sonship, an adoptive sonship participating in the natural sonship of Christ. The just Jew is inserted into Christ by faith and love, and the life of Christ flows through him, operating a true internal change, an ontological sharing in the sonship of the One who is to come.[4]

It is clear that St. Paul considers Israel's adoptive sonship a gift that Israel possesses precisely as the covenanted spouse of Jahweh, for he places it among those gifts Israel received quite apart from the Church or the preaching of the gospel. Paul uses the term "adoption as sons" only four or five times, and generally speaking he applies it to the intimate relationship between God and the Christian created by sanctifying grace. But in Romans 9:3-5 he makes it evident that the Old Testament dispensation referred this gift to the Israelite.

In Old Testament thought Israel is God's son and must be free to serve God as He deserves to be served. The nation cannot be a slave precisely because it is sacred to Jahweh and must have liberty to express to God the reverence it feels. It is obliged to Jahweh in a special way and must serve Him as a son, observing the law and keeping the commandments.

While at first among Israelites there seems to be no distinction based on moral values concerning sonship, it was gradually realized that true sonship implied more than a racial bond, descent from Abraham. Those who observe the covenant are truly God's sons, and the Lord has pity on those whose filial fear motivates them to obey His mandates. "As a father has compassion on his children, so the Lord has compassion on those who fear him, for he knows how we are formed; he remembers that we are dust" (ps. 102 [103]:13-14). Those who do not observe the law are false children, unfaithful to the family relationship.

The books of Sirach and Wisdom accent the sonship of the individual and the protection God offers to the pious. Sometimes the pious individual was evidently mocked for his confidence in this fatherly protection. "He judges us debased; he holds aloof from our paths as from things impure. He calls blest the destiny of the just and boasts that God is his Father. Let us see whether his words be true; let us find out what will happen to him. For if the just one be the son of God, he will defend him and deliver him from the hand of his foes" (Wisd. 2:16-18).

The very use of the word Israelite in Romans 9:4 emphasizes the fact that it is as kinsmen of Abraham that the Jews share God's paternal blessings, for the word implies that, as individuals, they share blessings granted to the nation as a nation.

In chapter 11 of the Epistle to the Romans St. Paul underscores the reality of the blessings conceded to Israel, adopting two images—the tree and its branches and the leaven in the dough—which accent the real internal effect produced by God's adoption.

The relationship of sonship to God in the Old Testament, however, is, as we have said, founded not upon supernatural union with God or on any sharing in His nature but in physical connection with the chosen people of God (Deut. 14:1; Isa. 1:2; Jer. 3:19). The Israelite could in some sense call himself the son of God even if he were actually unjust, as the wicked judges are called the sons of God in psalm 81 (82). At times the angels are called the sons of God, as in Job. 1:6; at times also a certain holy part of the Israelite people will be referred to as a son of God, as in 2 Samuel 7:14.

The Common Fatherhood of God

An individual never addresses God as his father in the Old Testament until we arrive at Ecclesiasticus—unless he is speaking in the name of the entire Israelite people. In the literature which was written after the Jewish exile, however, each individual just man may call God his father and speak to him in this fashion, as we read in Wisdom 2:13. But even here the reason for ascribing sonship to the member of the Israelite race is not any sharing in the divine nature but rather the Jewish origin or the personal holiness of the individual. This common fatherhood of God is fatherhood only in a broad sense. It is true that Jahweh has chosen this people from out of all nations to preserve the true notion of God and to favor them with His revelation. He cares for them, surrounds them with His love and rebukes them as a father does his child, but it is not so much the individual as the race which is the beneficiary of Jahweh's love. Frequently, too, in the Old Testament God's fatherhood is revealed in rather severe fashion.[5]

Fatherhood in the New Testament

According to the gospels, and to Christ's own words in the synoptics, God is the heavenly Father who looks after all creatures and provides for the lilies of the field and the birds of the air with paternal love. He also makes the sun to rise upon the sinners and the just alike. But the eternal Father is in a special sense the Father of those whom He calls to the kingdom founded by Christ. Those who fulfill the commandments and the beatitudes are called the sons of God in a special way, and they can be recognized as such by their works. The one who fulfills the will of the heavenly Father is a brother of Christ: "Behold my mother and my brethren! For whoever does the will of my Father in heaven, he is my brother and sister and mother" (Matt. 12:49-50). The just of the New Testament possess the kingdom which the Father has prepared from the beginning of the world, for if they are sons they are also heirs.

The fatherhood of God is one of the principal objects of Christ's teaching, and He stresses it in the one prayer which He Himself placed upon our lips. The Our Father is a prayer unique in Christian devotion, summing up the spirit of filial piety, tenderness, and trust with which His disciples are to approach God. It is only in the light of divine adoption that we can fully understand Christ's demands upon us: "Be ye perfect even as your heavenly Father is perfect." The confidence which the Christian is to have is based upon realization of the same fact. If the pagan lives in anxiety, this is understandable, since he does not realize that God is a solicitous and tender father who surrounds His children with loving care.

The fourth gospel contains so many references to divine adoption that one could say that St. John has appreciated this idea more fully than the other evangelists. In his gospel and in his epistles he teaches the fact of our divine adoption as well as the means by which this adoption takes place. It is obvious that the motive for this divine adoption is the ineffable love of the eternal Father: "Behold what manner of love the Father has bestowed upon us, that we should be called children of God; and such we are" (1 John 3:1). It is clear, too, that it is Christ who, having joined the natural son of God in hypostatic union with human nature, has merited for us to be called His brothers. "But to as many as received him he gave the power of becoming sons of God; to those who believe in his name" (John 1:12); "Everyone who believes that Jesus is the Christ is born of God" (1 John 5:1). To obtain this divine filiation we must be united through the sacrament of baptism with the visible word of God: "Jesus answered 'Amen, amen, I say to thee, unless a man be born again of water and the Spirit, he cannot enter into the kingdom of God'" (John 3:5).

The internal cause of our adoption is sanctifying grace itself, as John indicates in the same passage and Paul indicates in Romans 8:14: "For whoever are led by the Spirit of God, they are the sons of God," and in Galatians 4:6 "And because you are sons, God has sent the Spirit of his Son into our hearts, crying, 'Abba, Father.'" Our divine Lord's discourse after the Last Supper is thoroughly penetrated with this idea of God's fatherhood; throughout, Jesus refers to God as a father. It is through Him that we are to go to the Father. Philip, who has seen Jesus, has seen the Father, and Jesus will speak to us plainly of the Father. In his First Epistle to the Christians of Palestine, from which we have already quoted, St. John maintained the same position when he said: "Behold what manner of love the Father has bestowed upon us, that we should be called children of God; and such we are" (1 John 3:1). This is an extremely felicitous expression of St. John's, since he stresses the fact that not only are we called sons but are truly such. Clearly there is no value within human nature itself which could call for this adoption. It is an entirely free gift from the Father which He adds to our nature, and He is Father to the Christian in a way in which He is not Father to all men. As many as received Christ, He gave them the power of becoming sons of God, to those who believed in His name and were born not of blood nor of the will of the flesh nor of the will of man, but of God.

It seems evident that sonship is a special favor reserved for those who have faith in Christ. John teaches us also that whoever is born of God does not commit sin because His seed abides in him. In this the children of God and the children of the devil are made known (1 John 3:9-10). "Whoever is not just is not of God" (1 John 3:10). Whoever does good is born of God, whoever believes in Jesus Christ is born of God (1 John 2:29; 5:1). The essence of this divine adoption is not merely a juridical relationship or legal fiction. On the contrary, it is something approximating genuine generation from God, since it is clear from Scripture that He confers upon us a share in His divine nature, so that we possess, through grace, a nature similar to that which is proper to God; the divine nature itself is physically communicated to us. However, in distinction from the natural generation from the Father of the only-born Son, the Word, our sharing is finite, not necessary, accidental. Nevertheless Sacred Scripture bears witness to a true *consortium* with the divine nature, for St. Paul tells us that man becomes a new creature by baptism (Gal. 6:15), is re-created (Ephes. 4:24), becomes a new man (Ephes. 2:15). Paul also calls the just man the son who is born of God (Rom. 8:16). We are from God, St. John tells us (1 John 4:4). We are generated from God (1 John 5:1); we are not only called the sons of God (1 John 3:1), but we actually are so.[6]

The term of this generation is a son. In Sacred Scripture divine adoption is always referred to the Father: "they are the sons of God" (Rom. 8:15); "And because you are sons, God has sent the Spirit of his Son into your hearts, crying, 'Abba, Father'" (Gal. 4:6). The Father, as the Principle without principle, is the ultimate explanation of all paternity in heaven and on earth. Because our filiation has some likeness to the filiation of the eternal Son it is referred to the Father, and we are called the brothers of Christ (Matt. 12:49-50). Our sonship is referred to Christ not as to a father but as to one who merited this grace for us and who is Himself the exemplary cause of filiation, since He fulfills it in a divine and infinite fashion. However, divine adoption is referred to the Holy Spirit as to the principle by which God confers this gift upon us. When Paul speaks to the Romans and to the Galatians in an effort to liberate them from devotion to the Mosaic law, he has to remind them that they must now free themselves from those practices because they have not received the spirit of fear but of adoption as sons, in virtue of which they cry, "Abba, Father." To the Galatians he says that when the fullness of time had come God sent His son that He might redeem those who were under the law and that we might receive the adoption of sons. We are no longer slaves but sons (Gal. 4:4-7).

The Emphasis of Trent

The Council of Trent adds emphasis to the teachings of Sacred Scripture when it declares that our divine sonship results, as do justification and grace, from a physical and intrinsic principle. The foundation of our divine adoption is exactly that which makes us participate in the nature of God Himself, namely grace. Even in the Old Testament, as we have said, those who were children of God were so not because of the power of the Mosaic law but because of the power of the Messias who was to come, and because of the charity and faith with which the just expected Christ.

If our concept of grace is an adequate one, it embraces also the self-communication of the substance of God Himself, which is Uncreated Grace. Our generation, therefore, is not only from God but also from God as from a conjoined principle, for by indwelling in us He gives Himself to us. Because of this indissoluble connection between created and Uncreated Grace it is not possible to distinguish in scriptural texts whether created or Uncreated Grace is the formal reason for our adoption.[7]

Whose Sons?

With regard to the term of this filiation—that is, with regard to the precise question as to *whose* sons we are—we may point out that Sacred Scripture constantly refers our adoption to the Father. "And because you are sons, God has sent the Spirit of his Son into our hearts, crying, 'Abba, Father'" (Gal. 4:6). "Blessed be the God and Father of our Lord Jesus Christ, who has blessed us with every spiritual blessing on high in Christ" (Ephes. 1:3). It is, as we have said, the eternal Father who, as the Principle without principle, is the ultimate exemplar of all paternity in heaven and earth: "For this reason I bend my knee to the Father of our Lord Jesus Christ, from whom all fatherhood in heaven and earth receives its name" (Ephes. 3:14-15). Since our filiation is a similitude of the filiation of the first-born Son, it should be referred, as His is, to the eternal Father. "Jesus said to her, 'Do not touch me, for I have not yet ascended to my Father and your Father, to my God and your God'" (John 20:17).

We are called not sons but *brothers* of Christ in Matthew 12:48. Sacred Scripture refers our sonship to Christ indeed, but never as to a father; rather as to the meritorious cause and the exemplary cause of our adoption. For example, in Hebrews 2:10 we read: "For it became him for whom are all things and through whom are all things, who had brought many sons into glory, to perfect through sufferings the author of their salvation." This way of speaking, in which our adoptive sonship is always referred to the First Person of the Blessed Trinity and never to the Triune God as such or to the eternal Word or to the Holy Spirit, is absolutely constant if one excepts Hebrews 2:13, "And again, 'I will put my trust in him'; and again, 'Behold, I and my children whom God has given me.'" Even here one should recall that the term "God" generally refers to the Father and is not understood of the entire Trinity but only of the First Person. In the New Testament *ho theos* stands for the Father.

A New Status

Our divine filiation brings with it consequences of great importance for the Christian. We are made aware of our new status by the testimony of the indwelling Spirit. "The Spirit himself gives testimony to our spirit that we are sons of God" (Rom. 8:16). Because we are sons of God we are no longer timid servants of the law, submitted to the world, but are made free. "Now you have not received a spirit of bondage so as to be again in fear, but you have received a spirit of adoption as sons, by virtue of which we cry, 'Abba, Father'" (Rom. 8:15); "Now I say, as long as the heir is a child, he differs in no way from a slave, though he is the master of all; but he is under guardians and stewards until the time set by his father. So we too, when we were children, were enslaved under the elements of the world. But when the fullness of time came, God sent his Son, born of a woman, born under the Law, that he might redeem those who were under the Law, that we might receive the adoption of sons" (Gal. 4:1-5). We are brothers of Christ and are conformed to the first-born son of God. The spirit of Christ lives within us and moves us, "For whoever are led by the Spirit of God, they are the sons of God" (Rom. 8:14). We are heirs of God and co-heirs of Christ, for the first-born son is no longer the sole heir but has made us co-heirs; "But if we are sons, we are heirs also: heirs indeed of God and joint heirs with Christ, provided, however, we suffer with him that we may also be glorified with him" (Rom. 8:17).

Because we are adopted sons we have new tasks and duties. We must show faith in the Christ and love of God and observance of His commandments. We should hate the world of sin, and above all we should display fraternal charity. "In this the children of God and the children of the devil are made known" (1 John 3:10). "Now that your obedience to charity has purified your souls for a brotherly love that is sincere, love one another heartily and intensely" (1 Peter 1:22). The final results of our filiation are not yet fully manifested, but the culmination of this filiation, our inheritance, is grasped by hope, and one day we will experience its reality, a knowledge of God as He is in Himself, the glorification of our body and of the whole created world. "Beloved, now we are the children of God, and it has not yet appeared what we shall be. We know that, when he appears, we shall be like to him, for we shall see him just as he is" (1 John 3:2). "And not only it, but we ourselves also who have the first-fruits of the Spirit—we ourselves groan within ourselves, waiting for the adoption as sons, the redemption of our body" (Rom. 8:23).

Our divine filiation, as we have seen, is referred rather to the Father than to the Son or the Holy Spirit. Is this simply a question of appropriation?* If we take Scripture as it stands, it appears to imply some kind of special relationship to the Father. However, we should not so understand it as to destroy the unity of the divine essence and the divine action in the world.

The Early Fathers

Those early Fathers who recognized the fact of divine adoption speak of it from time to time as though it were the aim of the entire action of God in creation, for the Word was made man in order that man might become the son of God. Creation sets out from God and returns to the Father, passing through the Incarna-

* Appropriation is the attribution to one Person of the Trinity, because of its resemblance to His personal character, a work which is common to all three Persons. For example, we think of power as characteristic of the Father. The creation is a work of power; hence we assign it to the Father by appropriation.

tion, which sanctifies and redeems creation. The Son and the Holy
Spirit are as the instruments of the Father in our process of divinization, realized historically through the Incarnation. We become par-
ticipants of the Son through the Spirit, and we learn little by little
to receive Him and to prepare for the glorious perfection of the
beatific vision.[8]

St. Athanasius, who spoke so much of divinization, emphasizes
strongly that we become divinized only through the incarnation of
the Word of God. As corruptible beings we are infinitely distant
by nature from the nature of God. But He offers us a gratuitous
gift, a participation in the Word, who is the perfect, infinite Image
of the Father. It is by sharing in the nature of the Son that man
becomes the image of God, capable of knowing the Father in a
way similar to that in which the Word, the eternal Image, knows
His Father. To know the Father as the Word knows the Father
is to live a divine life, to live in eternal beatitude. The purpose of
the incarnation of the Word is to restore God's creation, wounded
by Adam's sin. When the Word became incarnate He restored to
man, by His death and resurrection, a share in the divine incorruptibility and immortality. Union with the Father, through sharing
in the Son, His unique Image, by means of the redemptive incarnation—this is the aim of God's activity in the world. There is only
one Son, the unique and perfect Image of the Father, perfectly
consubstantial with the Father; He alone fully knows the Father,
and He is able to share His knowledge with us. By sharing in the
Son, through grace, we are made sons in the unique Son. We are
all united in Him, and through Him we are united to the Father,
so that we may know the Father as our father.

Since the Son has taken on a genuine human nature including a
human body, sanctifying grace will be conformed to our human
and corporal condition. This human nature of ours, through contact
with the eternal Word, has been empowered to receive grace and
to be divinized. We are assimilated, as sons, to the Sonship of the
eternal Word. We are sons through the presence in humanity of

the first-born Son who was made man to act as a bond of union between us and the Father. It is He who sends His Spirit to us, and it is the Spirit who teaches us to speak with confidence to God as a son to his father. It is the Spirit who conforms us to the first-born Son.[9]

Although we are by nature conformed in some sense to God, since we are an image of God, it is only through grace that we are able to share in the Sonship of the eternal Word. Christ, who is consubstantial with the Father, became consubstantial with man. By becoming consubstantial with us Christ has assumed an ontological relationship with all humanity, which in some mysterious fashion is really included in Him. But this inclusion, resulting from the Incarnation, while essential, does not constitute our filiation properly so called. It is only a fundamental or radical filiation, and to fulfill itself it must be completed by grace, by the sanctifying action of Christ's humanity in His sacraments, especially the sacrament of baptism.

Our Double Relationship

Since the Incarnation we have a double relationship to the Son of God, a natural physical relationship and a new, supernatural relationship through grace and assimilation. The grace which makes us sons of God is twofold.

First there is the grace of baptism, which sanctifies us spiritually and communicates to us the Spirit of the Son. The eternal Word of God is already related to us according to the flesh before He communicates His Spirit in baptism. But it is only at baptism that we become the temples of the Holy Spirit and are united to Him in a supernatural union. This sharing in the Spirit relates us very closely to the eternal Word, for we become His brothers, and as brothers of the first-born Son we are then sons of the eternal Father. Our divine filiation is thus wholly in the order of grace and is, as we have said, an imitation of the real and substantial generation of the eternal Word by the Father. Since we are all quasi-generated from the Father, all Christians should be united in love and charity.

The second is that grace by which we are sanctified corporally through the eucharist. We should keep in mind that the Christian has in some sense a sharing in the humanity of Christ and through that sharing an accidental contact with His divinity. The humanity of Christ therefore serves as an instrument in the giving of the spirit of adoption. Hence, according to the thought of the Fathers, our radical relationship to Christ is realized at the moment of the Incarnation, but this radical relationship is only a potential adoption or affiliation. Our whole supernatural relationship takes place through Christ, through the mediation of the incarnate Word and through baptism. We are fully established in the Spirit when Christ, risen from the dead and become the principle of a new humanity, communicates the spirit of adoption to His faithful at baptism. We are the sons of the Father through Christ in the Spirit.

While the Latin Fathers speak more of the liberating function of the Saviour and of His grace, one can still find in them traces of this theory of divinization so common in the Greeks. Augustine maintains that our adoptive filiation is a gratuitous extension of the natural filiation of God-made-man whose co-heirs we are become. Christ is the prototype and the source of our predestination because, having become man in order to become our Head, He diffuses in His members His own grace and His own spirit.[10]

One should note also that in the Fathers, as in the liturgy, the name of Father is almost never given to any but the First Person of the Blessed Trinity. When it is given to another it is usually an obvious metaphorical expression. The Fathers explain our affiliation through a sharing in the natural generation of Christ Himself, which is certainly to be referred only to the Father. They describe our rebirth as Christians according to that general theory by which they see the Father as operating through the Son and the Spirit, or through the Son in the Spirit. It almost seems as though the Father has some special title to be called our Father, for He seems in a special fashion to be the author and the term of our spiritual regeneration. Nevertheless, the Fathers firmly maintain the axiom that the essence of God is one and His activity outside the divinity is one and common to all three Persons.

The Scholastics

When the scholastics discuss the fact of our divine affiliation they usually explain it as a gratuitous admission of man to the divine inheritance. God adopts man, rendering him suitable to be adopted by sanctifying grace, disposing him to share in the divine goods. Our divine filiation is considered to be a sharing in the divine nature by which man participates in the perfections which are exclusively proper to the nature of God. Hence man is deified, is adopted as a son and is ushered into the divine order of things so that his beatitude will consist in the knowledge and love of the infinitely perfect essence of God, a beatitude like that of the first-born son. Adoption is an absolutely gratuitous act of God, since man is constituted a son only through grace, which is itself absolutely and simply not due to man's nature, and, in fact, transcends the exigencies of any creature. Moreover, the communication of the divine nature to us through sanctifying grace, while it is genuine and physical, is nevertheless accidental and only analogical to the nature which is possessed by the first-born Son. Uncreated Grace does indeed unite us directly to the divine essence, but this union with the divine substance is an accidental union.

One may wonder exactly what part the gift of Uncreated Grace plays in constituting man an adopted son of God. In order to resolve the problem it may help to recall that created and Uncreated Grace imply one another. Hence the man who does not possess God indwelling, the Uncreated Grace, cannot be a son of God, for he would not possess created grace either, in this supposition. Uncreated Grace doubtless concurs in constituting man an adopted son of God. Yet he who possesses created grace by that very fact is an adopted son, since he is formally assimilated to the divine nature, and possesses the Uncreated Gift which grants a participation in the nature of the Father.

All Catholic theologians agree that the divine filiation is somehow given by sanctifying grace. But certain theologians seem to make too drastic a separation between the created and Uncreated gifts of grace, as if the divine inhabitation were merely a secondary formal effect of created grace, and as though the two were quasi-independent. If one does this, of course, various theories can arise concerning the formal constituent element of divine adoption.

Grace a Dispositive Cause

The man in grace possesses God, present and actuating his soul, as will be explained later in discussing the divine indwelling. This actuation by God is a communication of divine life which renders man a son. We call sanctifying grace an adequate dispositive cause, for we are opposed to those theologians who would claim that something must be added to grace to constitute man a son of God. The remission of sin and the right to the divine inheritance belong essentially to the very nature of grace. Grace excludes sin with an absolute and metaphysical necessity. By its presence alone sin is destroyed in the soul, for sin is the privation of grace. As to the right which man has to the eternal divine good, his inheritance, we believe that grace by its own internal finality leads to glory, for it is the beginning of divine life and by that very fact a right to the family inheritance in heaven.

The soul that has been adopted by God is sealed with a divine likeness, so that God is able to see there reflections of His own divinity, of His own personal traits. In the intelligence illuminated by faith God perceives reflections of knowledge and convictions like His own. In the will inflamed by divine charity He perceives an aptitude to grasp Him directly in the beatitude of heaven. Since grace makes a soul participate in the divine nature, God cannot but love it more than He loves the soul in sin, for He loves whatever reflections of His own perfections He beholds in the creature. Everything that increases the conformity of the creature to God and His divine Son intensifies God's love for it. Hence the adopted son is an object of great love on the part of the eternal Father. Inasmuch as we resemble the Word in sonship we ought also to resemble Him in our acts, draw inspiration from His activity, and conform our manner of acting and thinking to His so that our filial life becomes more and more like His.

Social Consequences of Adoption

At the same time our supernatural sonship makes it evident that Christians share one basic equality; all are brothers regardless of differences in culture, grace, language or nationality. This oneness also enables us to experience a continual sharing in satisfaction and merits, a circulation of life from one part of the Mystical Body to another. There is a constant interchange of prayer and merits among Christians, an exchange the more intense the more the Christian is assimilated to Christ, the first-born Son. The progress of each Christian concerns all, the holiness of the saints and their increase in sanctity are a source of benefit to all other members of the Mystical Body. The supernatural bonds which unite Christians among themselves as brothers of Christ are more real and intimate even than the bonds of the flesh, for through sonship all Christians are objects of the same adoption and the same eternal solicitude.

It is clear from this that it is our duty to reflect on the social consequences of our supernatural brotherhood. This dogma, which is based on the common adoption of the Christian by God, made so profound an impression on the early Christians that they conformed their lives entirely to it and in a great surge of love put all their goods in common. All opposition between races or nations or classes ought to disappear in the light of this doctrine; all jealousy, egotism and bitterness should be replaced by mutual support and assistance.

This doctrine should also be a source of profound confidence to the Christian soul, since it is obvious that God loves the adopted soul in a way that produces perfection within it. Our perfection and value are produced by God; they are not the cause of His love but are caused by His love. He communicates His treasures to us; He protects and cherishes us as children, and consequently we cannot call upon Him in vain. His love is essentially efficacious and creative of good within us, for it consists of much more than mere good will toward us. Whatever good God wishes for us He actualizes, so that His love becomes a source of continual benefits for us. Our duty is to reply to His love with a filial love, including a high order of delicacy and tenderness. Such a tenderness, of course, man could not possess naturally, since left to his own devices he would rather fear God than experience such affection for Him. It is the Holy Spirit which kindles in the soul of the just that movement of filial devotion by which they cry, "Abba, Father!" This is a love which we must translate into action so that we shall live perfectly the life of sonship.

NOTES

1. S. Many, "Adoption," *D.B.*, col. 232.

2. M. Schoenberg, "Huiothesia: the Adoptive Sonship of the Israelite," *A.E.R.* (1960), pp. 261-263.

3. H. Rowley, *The Biblical Doctrine of Election* (London, Lutterworth Press, 1953), pp. 33-39.

4. Schoenberg, art. cit., pp. 670-673. Cf. D. Theron, "Adoption in the Pauline Corpus," *Evangelical Quarterly* (1956), p. 7.

5. P. Van Imschoot, *Théologie de l'Ancien Testament* (Tournai, Desclée et Cie, 1954), Vol. II, p. 269.

6. J. Bellamy, "Adoption Surnaturelle," *D.T.C.*, col. 430.

7. F. Bourassa, "Adoptive Sonship: Our Union with the Divine Persons," *Theological Studies* (1952), pp. 309-336.

8. Irenaeus, *Adversos Haereses*, 3, 19, 1.

9. Athanasius, *Contra Arianos*, I, 9, *P.G.* 26, 28; *ibid.*, II, 59, *P.G.* 26, 272; *De Incarnatione Verbi et Contra Arianos*, 8, *P.G.* 26, 996; *Ep. Iv ad Serapionem*, I, 19, 20, *P.G.* 26, 573, 577. Cf. X. M. Le Bachelet, "Athanase," *D.T.C.*, cols. 2166-2174, and R. Bernard, *L'Image de Dieu d'après S. Athanase*, pp. 141-146 and de Bovis, *op. cit.*, pp. 120-121.

10. Augustine, *In Joa.*, tr. xi, 6, *P.L.* 35, col. 1478; tr. xii, cols. 1484, 1486; *De Civitate Dei*, xxi, 15, *P.L.T.* 4, col. 729. Cf. G. Ladner, "St. Augustine's Conception of the Reformation of Man to the Image of God," *Augustinus Magister* (Paris, Etudes Augustiniennes, 1954), pp. 867-878.

8

GOD INDWELLING THROUGH GRACE

WE HAVE NOW to examine the data of revelation to discover what it tells us concerning the modality of the inhabitation. We are not therefore interested in detailing the facts of revelation, but in drawing from that source all that we can learn of the nature of the indwelling, the causality which operates in it, and the mode of the inhabitation. Since this truth of the indwelling is the climax of the tract on sanctifying grace, and since it reveals to us the very heart of the divine gifts, we must explore it thoroughly. We should not expect, however, to find in revelation a systematic organization of data, for the apostles and the evangelists were not writing scientific treatises. Still, we can establish from revelation the limits which it imposes upon any theory of the inhabitation.

The first point to make is that divine revelation reserves this inhabitation to the souls of the just. We observe this clearly in the fourteenth chapter of St. John in which the evangelist puts in the mouth of Christ the words, "If anyone love me he will keep my word and my Father will love him, and we will come to him, and make our lasting abode with him." The advent of the Father and the Son is here promised to those who observe the commandments of God and who love Him. God was already present to the apostles and to those who were with Christ, with that ordinary presence by which He is present in all things. Now Christ says, "If anyone love me, the Father will love him, and we will come and take up our lasting abode with him." Clearly, Christ is promising a specifically new type of presence. He had already, in verse 16, promised the apostles that He would remain with them forever; now He extends this to all the just, to all those who keep his commandments (verse 23). This same emphasis on a new and special presence is found in the First Epistle to the Corinthians, chapter 6, verse 19, in which St. Paul says: "Do you not know that your members are the temple of the Holy Spirit, who is in you, whom you have from God, and that you are not your own?" Paul points out that the Holy Spirit will enter into the souls of the just so that they may become, properly speaking, a religious place, a place consecrated and dedicated to God. A temple was always considered in ancient literature as a place reserved to the gods. The souls of the just are now thought of as such.

They are said also to possess the Spirit. This emphasizes a second aspect of the inhabitation. Not only does the Holy Spirit dwell within man, but by this indwelling man is given a genuine possession of the Spirit, entering into a contact of mind and heart with Him. Paul stresses this when he says: "whom you have from God." Further, because man possesses the Holy Spirit he is in a particular way possessed *by* the Holy Spirit. He belongs no longer to himself but is of God. Paul is speaking to the just—that is, to Christians; he is urging them to avoid all sins which would drive out the indwelling Spirit. The contrast is between the Christian who is just and must remain just lest he lose the Holy Spirit, and the sinner who, because he is a sinner, does not have the indwelling Spirit. In this way Paul accents the fact that this inhabitation belongs to the just.

Continuing to explain the elevated state of the Christian, Paul says: "These things you were"—and he lists a number of sins—"these things you were in the past, but you were washed, you have been justified in the name of the Lord Jesus Christ and in the Spirit of our God." It is in these souls that have been washed and justified, cleansed in the name of our Lord Jesus Christ, our God, that the Holy Spirit dwells. The same idea is found in Romans, chapter 5, verse 5. Paul tells the Christians that their hope will not be confounded because charity, the love of God, is poured out in their hearts by the Holy Spirit who is given to them. One must analyze the character of gift here. Normally a gift is a good transferred into the possession of another because of an attitude of interior benevolence or love on the part of the giver. Paul, speaking of Christians in the state of grace, says that the Holy Spirit has been given over into their possession. We know from verses 2 and 3 that he is speaking of the just. He is addressing those who are justified by faith and who glory in the hope of the glory of the sons of God. Thus Paul implies once more that there is a new and a special presence reserved to the just.

Again we find that Paul has told the Romans that they are "in the spirit" (Rom. 8:9-10). The word spirit here could be with a small s (or in Greek with a small p, *pneuma*). By spirit Paul here means that the Romans, having been justified, are in mind and heart and will and choice under the directive influence of the Holy Spirit. Paul is positing an intimate nexus between "having the spirit of Christ," namely thinking and willing and choosing as Christ does, and the possession of a *Person,* the Holy Spirit. If one has the divine personality of the Holy Spirit within him, guiding and directing, and if one is sensitive to His guidance, then he is said to be living "in the spirit of God." He possesses the divine person, the Pneuma. Those who do not possess this divine person are living in the flesh. One is just only insofar as he possesses a Person. One possesses the created gifts and attributes of grace only insofar as the Uncreated Giver is there giving His gifts.

Grace Implies the Giver

Grace, then, is a gift which implies the presence of the Giver. The Giver is involved in the gift to such an extent that the gift cannot be handed over to the other unless the Giver Himself is involved, included, made present by it. The connection between justification and the sending of the Holy Spirit is closely analyzed in Galatians 4:6: "Because you are sons, God has sent the Spirit of his Son into our hearts crying, Abba." That is, because you are named, and are in very truth, the sons of God, having received divine adoption and filial attitudes, the Holy Spirit teaches you to regard God as a Father, who moulds you after the pattern of the family relationship to God, giving you a filial adoration, a filial trust, a filial confidence. With right you cry to God: "Father!" This same relationship is seen also in 1 John 4:16: "he who abides in love abides in God, and God in him." Those who love and obey the commandments, the divine vocation to sonship, adopt a filial attitude of love towards God. Expressing this in their relationship to their neighbor, they are in God and He in them. If God is in those who are living in charity, grace and obedience to His commandments, then He is not in those who are not living with this life. The special presence is reserved to the just.

This is the position taken by the Fathers in their insistence that the Holy Spirit is given at baptism, and that only those are just who maintain the unity with the Holy Spirit brought about by that sacrament. Baptism, which justifies man for the first time, is identified with the transmission of the gift of the Holy Spirit. He is not given and is not present to the unbaptized soul. Ignatius of Antioch in his letter to the Ephesians (9:2), calls the faithful "Christ-Bearers" and "God-Bearers."[1]   When he was treated by Trajan as though he were an evil demon he cried out: "Let no one call a God-bearer a demon!" To the question of Trajan, "Do you then bear the Crucified within you?" Ignatius answered, "We do."

We are truly Christ-bearers and God-bearers because we are Christians living in the fullness of faith; and this implies that we possess charity, grace, and the indwelling God. Tatian tells us that the Spirit of God does not dwell in all men but only in the just.[2]

St. Augustine makes the same point very clearly in his letter to Dardanus: "We must confess that if God be everywhere by His divinity, He is not everywhere by His inhabitation; one cannot apply to everyone the words of the apostle: 'Know you not that you are the temples of the Holy Spirit—that the spirit of God dwells in you?' You cannot apply this to everyone, but it must be said of some: He who has not the spirit of Jesus Christ does not belong to Jesus Christ."[3] He who does not belong to Jesus Christ, who is not in the state of grace, does not have the spirit of Christ, the Holy Spirit. Cyril of Alexandria declares: "If we have not the spirit within us, then we are in no wise the children of God; we are made children of God, we are made adopted sons, by the presence of the spirit; for how can we be sharers in the divine nature, if God does not dwell within us?"[4] The only way we can be sharers in the divine nature is through the presence of the Spirit who communicates this nature to us.

Later theologians, too, insist that the presence is reserved exclusively to the just. Suarez says in his book on the Trinity: "When God pours out on the soul the gift of sanctifying grace, it is not only these gifts but the divine persons themselves who enter the soul and begin to dwell there."[5]

The Council of Trent, speaking of attrition based on motives which include the fear of hell, declares "that attrition which comes to the sinner as he prepares for confession is a gift of the Holy Spirit who *does not yet* indeed dwell within him but moves him."[6] Sinful man has not the Holy Spirit inhabiting because this is reserved exclusively to the just. Leo XIII in *Divinum Illud* states: "Through baptism the unclean spirit having been driven forth from the soul for the first time, the Holy Spirit enters into the soul and renders it like unto Himself." In the same document the Pontiff says that "God dwells within the just soul as in His temple."[7]

St. Thomas is just as explicit in attributing the divine inhabitation to the advent of grace. He says that "the divine Persons are said to be sent insofar as they exist in a new way in someone. The divine

Persons are said to be given inasmuch as they are possessed by someone, but neither of these things can be said *except according to sanctifying grace.*" It is sanctifying grace which renders the divine Persons sent and possessed by man. For beyond the normal and ordinary presence of immensity, there is another special presence reserved for those who have grace, by which, in the famous Thomistic expression, God is present "as one known in the knower, and one loved in the lover." Note how carefully Thomas expresses the two aspects of inhabitation. The Holy Spirit dwells within man. This suggests a new mode of presence. But the Holy Spirit is also possessed by man. And this expresses a new mode of possession.[8]

So we can conclude with certainty that there is a new presence of the divine Persons reserved exclusively to the just, and from the way the Fathers and Sacred Scripture speak we can also conclude that it is the very substance of the divinity, God in His plenary reality, which is made present. From their continual contrasting of the created gifts of God with a Person, the very substance of the divinity, they are clearly arguing that nothing short of the divine substance itself is somehow joined to man's soul in a new and intimate union which surpasses all previous unions of which man had been capable.

Possession Through Baptism

The Fathers speak also of the possession of God through baptism. Aphraates, one of the early Fathers of the Church, says: "At baptism we have received the spirit of Christ. In that same moment in which the priest invokes the spirit, heaven opens and He descends. He broods over the waters of baptism, and they who are baptized take on the Holy Spirit, for the Holy Spirit is absent from all those born of the body until they come to the waters of regeneration. Then they receive the Holy Spirit."[9] He who lacks

this presence of the Holy Spirit is said to be either unbaptized
(in the state of original sin) or in the state of mortal sin. The
presence is reserved for those who have grace within their souls.
St. John Chrysostom says that through baptism we possess the
fountainhead of all our spiritual goods. We receive at baptism
the remission of our sins, participation in the spirit. We share
in the spirit. We have the spirit of "adoption and eternal life."[10]

It is well to recall at this point that the early Fathers always
associate the sacrament of penance with the sacrament of baptism.
Penance is regarded as a second baptism, so that if man is in the
state of mortal sin and approaches the sacrament of penance,
the Holy Spirit enters into his soul and possesses it. St. Cyprian
teaches that those who receive pardon in the sacrament receive
the Holy Spirit. He gives absolution to the penitent even before
he has had time to perform his canonical penance. He does
this that man may receive the Spirit and be encouraged to live
the Christian life, especially if he is facing imminent persecution.[11]

This is the tradition of the Church. Ambrose tells us that the
sinner is like the prodigal son: he is reconciled to the Church, he
receives the nuptial garment, sanctifying grace, and the sealing
of the Spirit.[12] The just need nothing but their justice to receive
the inhabitation. St. Jerome remarks that the priest who imposes his
hands on the sinner to reconcile him to the Church invokes the
return of the Holy Spirit. It is unquestionably the teaching of
revelation that with the advent of grace, either at baptism or
penance, there comes the Holy Spirit.[13] It follows that no one
can construct a theory to explain this inhabitation which would
require acts beyond those made by the one being baptized, which
would require more than the state of grace itself as a condition for
the inhabitation.

The terms of revelation are very clear with respect to the inhabitation. In the justified man God Himself comes to dwell.
This implies that the Trinity comes first of all willingly, and
secondly with the intention of remaining. The union between the

just soul and the divinity who inhabits it cannot be merely what we call a moral union, one of thought and affection. The presence of the Spirit cannot be the effect of one's act of thought and of will, since the sinner too is obviously quite capable of thinking of God. And although his thought or will renders God present to the sinner in the intentional or in the moral order, it does not bring him the substance of God newly present.

It is quite different with the union that is effected in the order of grace. Somehow this must be a uniting of soul with the very substance of the Trinity, out of which arises a new relationship of the soul to God. The foundation for this new relationship to the Trinity is, of course, sanctifying grace. There is here a certain reciprocal causality. Having passed from the state of sin into the state of grace, man receives a new absolute reality, sanctifying grace, which establishes a new relationship between him and God. But the change, as we have emphasized in an earlier chapter, is in man, and not in God.

A New Capacity

Since the substance of the divinity is already present to man, how can God become newly present to man in grace? The problem here arises out of the data of revelation that (a) there is in the just the substantial presence of the substance of divinity; (b) this presence of the substance of the Trinity is specifically different from any other presence had without grace; (c) this substantial presence endows us with a new capacity to know and to love God, for revelation speaks of a possession, and all possession means the capacity to use and enjoy. The just man is therefore rendered newly capable of enjoying the Holy Spirit, capable of a new kind of knowledge and a new kind of love. These two aspects must be balanced; one cannot explain one and ignore the other. The taking possession of God occurs between man as a person and the personal God, between the living, spiritual, intellectual soul and the living, spiritual, intellectual, loving God. The Holy Spirit is present to man as the most welcome guest of the soul. Man is then enabled to enter into conversation with Him, with all the intimacy, the sharing of goods, that friendship implies. Man shares his goods by *agape,* effective, efficacious love for the neighbor; God shares His goods with man by divinizing man and rendering him a sharer of His own divine nature. So we have to explain not only presence, but possession. Presence must be substantial and specifically new; possession must be new.

St. John and St. Paul are tireless in expounding the element of possession. With grace and the indwelling, they say, there comes a community of thought and love between the Godhead and man. There comes a circuminsession, so to speak, of thought. Man's thoughts are known to God, God's thoughts are known to man and, as with two people who love each other, thoughts flow from one to the other, colored by nuances, the tone of each personality.

A delicate and divine familiarity is made possible to man by the soul's presence to God and the soul's possession of God. An affectionate intimacy arises for man to cultivate and increase. And all the while the soul is brought into a unity of love, forming with the Godhead a loving "we." It is always the delight of lovers to speak of "our" love, for love is a circumambient element which preserves and unites them—an erosphere, so to speak, having almost an independent existence. Such a love unites the family— mother to child, husband and wife to child. Thus between the soul and God grace establishes a unity of mind and heart, and so essential an aspect of the inhabitation is this unity that no explanation of the presence of God can afford to ignore it.

Along with the inhabitation the soul receives a created gift distinct from the Person. But this gift involves the Giver. Try as we may, we human beings never succeed in impregnating whatever we give with the essence of our personality, so that it comes to the recipient reflecting perfectly our thoughts and desires. But God is able to achieve this in a substantial fashion, for with the gift of grace there is drawn in, immediately and inevitably, the divine Giver Himself. The nature of the gift given, the created gift of grace, is such that it cannot exist without the presence, the support, and the loving donation of the Giver Himself. God has achieved a mode of union impossible to us, even with those we love the most.

Grace an Accident

Since this gift of grace is added to a nature already substantially complete, we know that, philosophically speaking, it cannot be a substance but must be an accident. We know also from revelation that this created grace *inheres* in the soul, as Trent teaches, is capable of increase, and is therefore an absolute accident. We may conclude, therefore, that grace is a created, spiritual, absolute, qualitative accident, an accident which inheres in the soul, empowering the soul to supernatural acts, and which bears a proportion to man's end—the happiness proper to God, the beatific vision of heaven. But we will speak more of this in another chapter.

A New Union of Love

The new union of love is different from the love that creatures lacking grace would have for God. God gives man a share in His own proper intellectuality by which He knows Himself and loves Himself. In this life man will not see God as He is in Himself, but he has the radical capacity for this vision, and one day he will possess it. Nevertheless man has already adopted the attitudes of God through faith. Having entered into the divine viewpoint, he has come into contact with innumerable truths the existence of which he could not otherwise have known or even suspected. The whole area of human intelligence—and this includes man's outlook on the world of values, persons, things, activities—has been expanded and clarified by these truths.

Man in the state of grace has also the power to love God directly in a new way, to know and to hope in the God who has committed Himself to him. And all through his life there is an invitation to man on the part of God to increase this objective, intimate union. Since the presence involved is that of a Person, it is an invitation to a reciprocity of persons. It is an invitation to accept our relational character, for we are modeled on the Trinity, which too is relational. So we are ordained by God to move out in love and sympathy and knowledge to other human beings, other images of God.

It is only to the soul in grace that God so delivers Himself. He is known to other people, but He is delivered to be possessed in this intimacy of joy and friendship only to the soul in grace. If such a one is so unfortunate as to fall into mortal sin, he does not lose the endless series of truths about God which he has painfully and laboriously acquired, but he loses his close personal association with God; he cannot speak to Him with the intimacy of a friend, open to Him his dispositions, thoughts, desires, or share any longer in that reciprocal movement of being. The operations of the just soul terminate in God Himself, in faith, in hope and in love. These operations are not yet perfect, for although faith interprets every aspect of reality, giving one a connaturality with the good, still one cannot yet see the divine One for whom he is ordained. The heart pants after the living water, the presence of the Beloved is given, but full communication with Him is not. One is still dependent upon the propositional statements He has given in faith, and upon the Person behind them, for every word of faith terminates in the person Christ, the Substantial Revelation of God. It is Christ who interprets man's existence to him, yet man is constantly reaching out for more knowledge of the divinity. Even the mystics attain only a dark knowledge of God, so that faith always tends towards the fullness of vision. One can love God in this life, but one cannot know full fruition.

We have therefore to offer an explanation of the Trinity indwelling in our souls in a way which will explain all of these aspects: a specifically new presence, an objective union of knowledge and love, a new type of possession impossible to the sinner. And basic to them all the question: How is the God of immensity, who is present everywhere, newly present to the just man?

NOTES

1. *P.G.* 5, 652.
2. *Adversus Graecos*, 13, *P.G.* 6, 835.
3. *Ep. 187 ad Dardanum*, Caput V, *P.L.* 33, 237-838.
4. *In Joannem*, 9, *P.G.* 74, 260.
5. 12 B, c. 5, n. 8.
6. Denzinger 898.
7. Denzinger 1063.
8. *S.T.* I, q. 43, a. 3, e.
9. *Demonstrationes*, 6, 14, *P.S.* I, 291.
10. *In Actus Apostolorum*, 40, 2, *P.G.* 60, 285.
11. *Epist. LVII*, 4: *CV* 3, 653.
12. *De Poenitentia*, II, 3, 18, *P.L.* 16, 522.
13. Jerome *Dial. cont. Lucifer*, 8, *P.L.* 23, 167.

9

THE MODE OF GOD'S INDWELLING

(I)

THERE IS NO WAY of explaining precisely how God becomes newly present to the just man which has met universal acceptance among theologians. That God is present is clear to all, but to explain how this happens is very difficult, since one enters the realm of the mysterious in which much must be uncertain. At best theologians can offer what seems to them a more or less probable explanation, and that is what we will attempt here. There are four different explanations which have their adherents among Catholic thinkers, and we shall touch on all of them in this chapter, but the one to which we subscribe is that of Maurice de la Taille, which has the rather forbidding name of "the created actuation" theory. It implies that God acts somewhat as a formal cause to man's soul, so we shall have to examine a bit the notion of what a formal cause usually is and does.

The Presence of Immensity

The reason theologians begin the study of this problem with a discussion of causality is that they all recognize that whenever and however God becomes present, He does so by *causing*. When

God causes anything to exist, He at once becomes present to that thing by the ordinary presence we call the presence of immensity. Thus God is present even to the sinner by His ordinary presence of immensity, causing him to continue to exist; but He is not present to the sinful man by the new presence He has in relation to the just. Now if God is always present where He exerts His causality, it might be that He exerts a new type of causality with regard to the just, and this would offer us an explanation of how and why He is present in a new way to the just and to them alone.

Efficient Causality

Our task now is to explore the data of revelation to determine whether some new type of causality will explain the divine inhabitation. We begin this search knowing that the presence of immensity, by which God is present to all things, arises out of efficient causality —i.e., God's action in producing being. Since revelation has very clearly indicated to us a specifically new presence of God in the souls of the just, we might first ask whether *efficient* causality, which acts by producing something, could explain this new special presence. If it is true that the mode of God's presence follows upon the mode of His causality, then one might suspect that if God is present to all men by efficient causality, as by His action He has caused them to exist, His presence in the just cannot be explained by efficient causality, for this new presence is not different with respect to *degree* but is a different *kind* of presence. We are led to inquire, then, whether other types of causality may not explain the divine inhabitation.

Material Causality

Obviously we cannot appeal to material causality, for God cannot be a material cause, since a material cause is always an inferior principle perfected by the application of a form. Neither can we explain God's new presence through final causality, because the notion of final causality implies that the final cause, which exercises its causality by attracting man, is extrinsic to man. Final causality is always an extrinsic causality, but we are trying to explain something which acts within man and which is present to him.

Formal Causality

There is left formal causality, or in the strict sense of the term, a form which donates itself to matter. Formal causality is the term applied to the action of a form which contributes, or gives itself in some fashion, to matter. The form, a perfecting principle, donates itself to another principle which is perfected by it—the matter, or potential principle, the perfectible principle. In the human person, for example, the soul is the perfecting principle, or form, for it gives existence, perfection and specification to the body, and the body is human because the form which joins the matter is a *human* form. Formal causality also exists in an accidental fashion—that is, when something already constituted in its substantial reality receives an accident, as when white hair becomes colored red. Accidents are forms which modify and inhere in the substance and are communicated to it through formal causality. In donating, communicating, giving itself to matter, the form becomes limited by it, contracted to the potencies of the matter. But since God cannot possibly be limited and contracted to the potencies of the human being, a limited, finite creature, He cannot be a formal cause. It might seem that formal causality is excluded.

Moreover, as we have already seen, God does not enter into a substantial union with the Christian. That is what has taken place with the sacred humanity of Christ: the divine nature having entered into substantial union with the human nature of Christ, Christ is God. In the case of the inhabitation, man does not, of course, become God, although he is divinized, changed, qualified, lifted to a new order of being and consequently of activity. We are certain, then, that there is no strict substantial or hypostatic union between man and God in the inhabitation, and no ordinary formal causality.

To press the matter further, we know that when a form, or perfective principle gives itself to another principle it enters into a substantial union, so that what results from the donation of form to matter is higher in perfection than either the form or the matter alone. The third thing resulting from the union is more complete, more perfect, than were either of the two components of the union. Now it is clear that there cannot exist a composite, made up of God and man, which is more perfect than God. Under the pressure of such a joining, the personality of man would dissolve. What would be left would be God hypostatically joined to a human nature, another Christ, but it would not be a human person. God's purpose in granting man the inhabitation is that man should survive to be inhabited.

Quasi-Formal Causality

Having excluded efficient causality, since it gives only a difference of degree; final causality, since it is essentially extrinsic; and material causality, since God cannot be a material cause, we now exclude strict formal causality, since this would imply a substantial union between man's soul and the divinity in which man's personality would disappear. We are left, it seems, with a type of causality *resembling* formal causality, but without the imperfections manifest when creatures are the formal cause. We are left with an analogous formal causality, or quasi-formal causality.

But does revelation move us in this direction? Yes, because Scripture and the Fathers suggest that there is a mysterious kind of formal causality at work in the inhabitation. Now if the causality is at all formal, then the most intimate union is possible between the substance of the divinity and the substance of man. If God should act as a super-substantial form to man's soul, he would be present to man in a new and most intimate way, specifically different from the mode in which He is present to all other creatures.

The Greek Fathers and St. Paul suggest to us that there is a very strong analogy between the presence of God in the just soul and the presence of a form to its matter. In the Pauline theology of justification there is a double emphasis. There is first the element stressed in the Epistle to the Romans, the incorporation of the Christian into Christ. Man is baptized into Christ, becomes a living member of His mystical body, dies and is reborn into Him. But there is a second concept of justification in Paul, a second emphasis at least, and it is the idea that those who are the sons of God, those who are justified, are led by the Spirit. This second concept identifies the state of justification with being "in the spirit." A close examination of the text reveals that St. Paul speaks of two "spirits," one of which is a proper noun. To be "in the spirit" flows directly from the fact that man possesses the Spirit—i.e., the Holy Ghost. Man is justified if he possesses the indwelling Spirit. The spirit conceived as an internal quality which transforms the soul and sanctifies man is what we call the created gift of sanctifying grace.

But the relationship between the two concepts in St. Paul is not simply one of contiguity. The created gift results from the presence of the Uncreated Gift. Man is "in the spirit," led by the Spirit of God—sanctified, justified, transformed interiorly, possessing created sanctifying grace—only because he has the Holy Spirit. The principal part of justification is the work of the Holy Spirit Himself, not that of the created gift of grace, as is clearly seen in Romans 8:9 and in Ephesians 1:13. "To be sealed" by the Spirit is to possess the interior quality of sanctifying grace; the one who does the sealing is the Holy Spirit.

The Self-Gift of God

The Greek Fathers rightly insist that the only reason man is deified is that God has poured Himself into the soul. If man is to be deified, the seal imprinting itself must be the very substance of God Himself, for it requires God Himself to communicate divinity to man.[1] The analogy in the Greek Fathers is carried even further than that in St. Paul. Arguing that this seal is like that applied to liquid wax, they maintain that the soul is always liquid and will immediately lose the imprint unless the impressor—the Spirit, God—is constantly present, donating Himself. If the seal (God) is removed from the soul, the imprint (created grace) will vanish. Therefore, they insist, one must have the immediate presence of God—the presence of God unmediated by any creature.

The Greek Fathers also elaborate this theme when they describe the Holy Spirit as a painter or sculptor. But He is wholly unique as an artist, for He engraves or paints His own image on the soul, not by using a tool or a brush, but by applying Himself (much as a form does to matter). The Holy Spirit is at once the pattern *according to which* man is to be sculptured, the agent *doing* the sculpturing, and the substance out of which He sculpts the image in man. He paints by *donating* His substance to the soul. And in a still further analogy the Fathers say that the soul is anointed. The Holy Spirit is like perfumed oil. But He not only applies the oil to man as an efficient cause, He is Himself the oil applied, and so there is an identity between the ointment applied to the soul and the One applying. In all their explanations it is always this direct, unmediated donation of the Godhead to man's soul which the Greek Fathers stress.[2]

Obviously such causality as they describe cannot be efficient causality, for an agent, an efficient cause, does not communicate its *substance*. When a man acts upon a piece of marble as agent, an efficient cause, there does not necessarily result a resemblance to the artist, but the marble takes the form of whatever idea the artist had in mind. This is not what happens with the divine sculpture of the Holy Spirit. He causes His effect, not by acting exteriorly upon man but by giving Himself; hence the image that arises is a likeness to Himself, a divinization. And this is what we mean by formal causality—a self-giving of the form to the matter.

Another image popular with the Greek Fathers is that of perfume. If a bottle of rose perfume is opened, the scent of roses diffuses itself into every corner, giving its specifically roselike smell. The perfume surrenders what it has of perfection, its specific type of perfection, communicating itself to the air. This idea of self-diffusion, self-giving, emphasized so often in the Greek Fathers, suggests again the idea of formal causality. The Spirit does not give something other than Himself but causes to arise in man a created likeness to Himself by giving Himself. Because grace is an image, a likeness of God, it can arise only if no creature intervenes—i.e., only by direct *self*-giving.

The form in donating itself, communicating itself, shares its perfections with the matter. This it does, not by acting upon the matter from the outside but by totally penetrating it from within. The soul does not make the body to act as an instrument except *by informing* it and communicating to it its specific type of perfection, namely, intellectuality. Because we possess the personal Spirit of God we possess *einai pneumatikos*, a share in God's nature. Nowhere in St. Paul or in the Greek Fathers do we find the idea that *because* man possesses the created gift of grace God is present to him. Man could not be in the state of sanctifying grace without the indwelling Spirit, for the only way sanctifying grace can arise is through God's donation of Himself.

One must keep well in mind that grace is a creature, a limited being, while the prime gift is the Uncreated Gift who by donating Himself brings grace into being. This is the doctrine of St. Cyril of Alexandria, Athanasius, and many others. The transformation that takes place in man is explainable in its origin by the fact of the divine Giver communicating Himself. Unless we choose to ignore the whole of patristic tradition we cannot elaborate a theory of grace without integrating the conclusions formulated by these great theologians. We must hold that the divine Persons contribute themselves by a mysterious adhesion to the soul, thus rendering it holy, an adopted child of God, for created grace alone could not deify man. Since we know that it does precisely this, it is clear that it does so only through the giving of the divinity to our souls. But if, *per impossibile,* created grace could arise by a method other than the giving of God to the soul, it would still not be able to deify man, because it is a creature and no creature can deify. The only way a deiform quality can arise in the soul is by the action of one who is divine impressing Himself immediately and directly upon it.[3]

Certainly, insofar as grace is a creature it is produced by God's efficient causality, as are all creatures. But because grace is the only creature which is the supernatural image of God Himself, it can arise only by a combination of efficient causality and another type of causality, which leans emphatically in the direction of formal causality. We think we may legitimately state that God inhabits the soul in such a fashion that He may be said permanently to actuate, or act as a form towards, the soul. He functions somewhat as an act to the potency of the soul. Sanctifying grace not only grants us a formal, created sharing with the divine nature, it also confers on us a terminative *consortium,* a new relationship to the divinity which we call the inhabitation. This union between the substance of the soul and the substance of the divinity is an immediate, ontological union, but of course not a substantial union.

The new and special presence of God is to be conceived as a permanent actuation of one's soul by God Himself. The new presence is real, is not merely in the order of thought, of affection —that is, the moral order. The technical description of this theory (which, as we have said, is that of Maurice de la Taille) is "created actuation by Uncreated Act." In terms of it God, the Uncreated Act, actuates man's soul and effects a created actuation. The actuation within man's soul is the created gift, grace. This, it will be noted, is a translation into philosophical terms of what the Greek Fathers have written: the seal is the Uncreated Act, the sealing is the actuation, the imprint is the created actuation which arises in the soul, or sanctifying grace. Or, in other words, the actuator is God Himself, the one actuated is man. Grace is the result of the action of God, the Uncreated Actuator.[4]

As an example consider how, since man's soul is gifted with intellectual life and gives itself to the body, we have body, soul and a third thing: the intellectual life arising in man. This intellectual life is neither soul nor body, but something contributed to man from the soul, because the soul possesses intellectual life. The three factors in the *human* composite are soul (the form), body (the material principle) and life (the formal effect produced when the soul donates itself to the body). In the analogy, where God actuates or acts somewhat as a form, we again have three factors: God (the formal principle), the human soul (which here acts as the material, determinable, perfectible principle) and sanctifying grace (the formal effect produced in man's soul when God donates Himself as a quasi-form to the soul, the perfectible principle).

Just as when the intellectual soul gives itself to the body there arises in man the capacity to think and to choose—in other words, intellectual life—so, when God gives Himself to the soul there arises in the soul sanctifying grace, which is neither the soul nor God but a created, formed effect. No analogy could be perfect here; ours indicates that there are three factors involved: the human soul, God the actuator, and the created reality grace, which arises as a result of the donation of God to the soul. The process clearly involves a union between two substances. To repeat, sanctifying grace can make man an image of God, a son of God, an heir to heaven capable of the beatific vision, because it is not a reality totally independent of God. It can arise only through the self-gift of God to the soul. The special nature of grace is not explained by the fact that God *produces* it. God also produces cats, celery and fennel. The reason grace divinizes is that it is made through God's self-donation to man. This is the result of the immediate impact, the immediate joining, the non-mediated presence of the substance of God to the substance of the soul.

Although the two terms man and God are substantial, the union should not, as we have noted, be called substantial because this term is a technical one reserved for a union of another type. The union of grace is an accidental union between two substances in which the bond of union is *grace*, itself a created accident. The justified soul is united ontologically to the very reality of God Himself, not to an idea of God, nor to a creature made by God.

A Super-substantial Form

The three divine Persons are possessed by and had within the creature, the Holy Spirit becoming, as it were, the vital principle of the just soul. This is an expression much favored by St. Irenaeus, who refers to the Holy Spirit as a super-substantial form. He declares that the soul without grace is like the body without its soul; without the soul man's body is not human, is incapable of functioning in the intellectual order; so also man's soul, if he has not the state of grace, is deprived of its form, its soul, and cannot act in the divine order. The Holy Spirit is, as it were, the form of a form, the soul of the just man's soul.

As we have already seen, we cannot speak of proper information of the substance of the soul by the divinity. But the expression "created actuation by Uncreated Act" is still a licit one to explain the traditional images of the inhabitation. We find something similar to this even in earlier theologians. Peter Lombard, for example, affirmed the union of the human will to God in such wise that divine power is appropriated by the human will and made its own, clearly a type of information. Alexander of Hales insisted upon some type of information. Lessius, the great Jesuit theologian, taught that the divinity communicates itself to us as the principal form according to which we are called the sons of God, and he insisted that the created gifts are only the *bonds* of the union between God and the soul. Petavius, the great patristic theologian, held that the Holy Spirit communicates Himself, pouring Himself into the just, and is as it were a form by which men are rendered pleasing to God[5] and adopted sons of God. The other great patristic scholar, Thomassinus, maintained a somewhat similar doctrine.[6]

For the purpose of order we must remember that there are certain presuppositions of revelation which we cannot ignore in discussing the inhabitation. First, there is an intimate connection between the created gift of grace and the Uncreated Gift itself; secondly, God is in no sense a strict formal cause to the soul; and thirdly, God arrives in the soul owing to a previous disposition of the soul toward His possession. Since no form ever comes to matter or a perfectible principle until it is disposed to receive the form, it follows that if God is to come to the soul, then the soul must be disposed to receive Him. Now sanctifying grace we consider the adjustment, the disposition, the habilitation to receive God, but we must also explain the insistence of the Greek Fathers on the substantial character of the two terms.

Since it is the substance—the immediate, direct, total reality of God—which is united to the soul in the inhabitation, we can begin by saying that any theory of the inhabitation which explains God's presence as simply producing in man a new idea of God or a created sharing in His nature is not sufficient. Revelation does not simply say that man becomes a sharer in the divine nature. It says that God is given to him to possess.

We cannot affirm, either, that justification, though it is consequent to the Uncreated Gift, is independent of created grace. As we have already noted, the Council of Trent declared that the unique (inherent) formal cause of justification is grace. But in stating that there is only one formal cause of justification the council did not deny that the Holy Spirit may be a quasi-formal cause. The state-ment was aimed at that "double justice" theory of the theologians of Cologne, already mentioned, by which they hoped to placate the Lutherans. First they said, as we shall recall, that there is sanc-tifying grace, an inherent formal cause of justification, and secondly, that there is the "imputed justice" of Christ. One would be truly constituted just only if he had sanctifying grace *and if* the merits of Christ were imputed to him. The council replied against this theory.

In our theory, however, sanctifying grace itself implies and re-quires the presence of the Holy Spirit, for sanctifying grace is the ultimate disposition to the Uncreated Gift. We do not say that the Holy Spirit is an *inherent* formal cause; He does not inhere as an accident, because He is not an accident. Moreover, it would be im-possible for us to conceive a complete disparity between these two gifts; we could not understand the presence of the Holy Trinity to the soul if the soul were not first disposed by an interior mutation for this presence by sanctifying grace. Nor is God present simply as an efficient cause producing sanctifying grace, for then one would have God present by means of a created effect. It would not be an immediate presence of the substance, but a presence medi-ated by a created effect.

Proof that God is a Quasi-formal Cause

Our method of procedure in proving that God is a quasi-formal cause will be to analyze the conditions metaphysically required for the possibility of supernatural merit. And first we ask: what happens when man merits? In the meritorious activity of the just, man places acts which are proportioned to—which have as their term—eternal life, the possession of God Himself, the Supreme Good. Man's meri-torious acts are efficacious motions towards perfect beatitude, the beatific vision, but they are also genuinely *man's*. They are not produced by another within him (in which case it would be the other who merits) but flow out of his elevated nature, his essence, his active potency, the will. Still, they must also be proportioned to a *divine* good. Therein lies the problem. How can any act produced by a free, created, finite, human will be intrinsically proportioned to a *divine* good?[7]

An act of this nature, it seems, clearly implies a previous union between the human agent and God. If the human agent is an insufficient, non-proportioned principle, then he must be united with a higher agent to produce the higher effect. But human nature of itself is not proportioned to a divine good, and so must be united to a higher agent, God, who is proportioned to this good and who somehow lends His power to man. From the union of these two agents there is then constituted one complete principle, adapted to the effect to be produced.

The meritorious act, since it ends in the life of God Himself, heaven, transcends the proper forces of any creature, even of so glorious a creature as sanctifying grace. Since the actions of a being follow upon its constitution or its nature, an action which attains to the divine good of the beatific vision must involve a special, a divinized, nature in the agent. One might offer an objection here. "An agent which is elevated by sanctifying grace is already constituted an adequately proportioned principle of meritorious acts. Hence this actuation by God Himself is completely unnecessary." But created grace is still a creature, and the effect we are seeking, heaven, is the Uncreated Goodness of God Himself. In the intuitive vision, God Himself, in His substance, directly unites Himself to man's intelligence and actuates it. God is so immanent to man's intelligence that man knows Him immediately, as He is in Himself, a type of knowledge naturally proper to God alone. Consequently, it seems impossible, even with the aid of sanctifying grace, for man to produce this knowledge.

The meritorious act demands a stable and permanent union between man, the agent, and God. If God ordains man to the beatific vision, then certainly He must provide a lasting, stable power to produce the acts which lead to it. It does not seem fitting that man should be disposed only on those occasions when he performs meritorious acts. Existence is given for action and is adapted to the acts of the being. If man is ordained to intellectual life, he is permanently adapted by an inner principle to intellectual life. Similarly, if he is ordained by God to the beatific vision, he should be permanently adapted intrinsically to produce the acts which end in the beatific vision. To be permanently so ordained he must have within him an active power to produce meritorious acts, and this active power he acquires through his union with *God* in stable fashion, since no creature could adapt him for this vision, or for the meritorious acts which lead to it.

A permanent union of this nature seems to demand a permanent actuation of the human will by God Himself to allow man to merit. The addition of the created virtue of charity, or the created gift of grace, to man's will does not seem to be sufficient for this. Somehow man must appropriate the divine power and goodness and force itself.

Now the proximate principle of a meritorious act is not the intelligence but the will, for it is only because man's act is free that it can be meritorious. Consequently it would seem that the will itself should be actuated by God, joined immediately to God, "informed" by God, intrinsically united to Him.

Would not a purely *extrinsic* union between God and the will suffice? Could not God, the principal cause, use man's will as an instrumental cause, with the two as one principle producing the meritorious act? The higher agent, God, would then elevate the will (instrument), so that man could be said to be in some sense a genuine cause of his free act, and yet the free act would be on the divine level, for the principal cause would be God. Thus when God moves the priest to the eucharistic consecration He uses the priest as the instrument. But a union of this kind does not suffice for the demands of the meritorious act, because in this hypothesis the free act, *insofar as it is divine*, supernatural, divinized, would not be man's. The act as free and supernatural must flow from *man's will*. We might also inquire if it is even conceivable, philosophically, that the human will, precisely as free, should be an instrument? Is the will not always the principal cause of its action?

God alone is the agent truly proportioned to produce an act meritorious of eternal life, an exclusively divine good, and yet man alone is the agent of his meritorious acts, as free and supernatural. The conclusion would seem to be that man's will, if it is to produce supernatural acts, must identify itself with, possess and appropriate as its own, the divine strength, the divine force. This vital state arises when God applies Himself to the soul to deify man, divinizing his free life by allowing him to appropriate the divine power. Man's will is a creature; the actuator, He who donates Himself, is the Uncreated God. The communication or self-donation of God, the actuation, is created. The possession is created, the possessed is Uncreated; the possessor is man's will, which remains distinct from God but enriched by the divine wealth. The theory of actuation thus reconciles two apparently impossible terms. In man's will is a created actuation by which the potency of the will is actuated in the supernatural order by the divine goodness. This is the created habit of charity by which the divine power is interiorly communicated to the will, by which man is made powerful with the power of God.

The situation differs from that of a miracle worker who raises a body from the dead. The miracle worker has no power to revivify bodies even inchoatively, or initially. Since this potency does not exist in him it cannot be perfected. The human will, however, has a proportioned and adequate object, namely, the possession of human goods. Because of the possibility of the human will for human or natural beatitude, it has within it a potency which God can perfect, so that it can possess God Himself. In acting here, God perfects the will, as a will, expanding its capacity for good. When God is resolved to unite Himself to the human will, His divine power finds ready in man a co-natural power for good which it can expand and perfect, so that the new term towards which God leads the will is not heterogeneous. Man is meant to be happy with a human happiness, but he has the power as a human being to know and to love God. There is nothing contradictory, then, in God's taking this knowledge and saying: "I will give you a better kind of knowledge—vision; and I will give you a better kind of love by which I will perfect your power to love me by uniting myself with you."

Man is ordained to know God by conceptual knowledge, to possess the world, to possess good, to possess God in the world. Through grace God reaches to expand this capacity so that man's possession and knowledge of Him may be new and more perfect.

NOTES

1. P. Gächter, "Zum Pneumabegriff des hl. Paulus," *Z.K.th.* (1929), pp. 345-408.

2. See the examples used by P. Galtier, whom we follow here, in his *L'Habitation en nous des trois Personnes* (Paris, Beauchesne, 1933), pp. 201-209 and *passim.*

3. See Cyril of Alexandria, *Thesaurus,* assertio 34, *P.G.* 75, 1114. Cf. Athanasius, *Ep. ad Serapionem,* n. 23, *P.G.* 26, 586.

4. M. de la Taille, "Actuation créée par acte incréé," *Rech. de Science Religieuse* (1928), pp. 253-268, and "Entretien Amical d'Eudoxe et de Palamède sur la grace d'union," *Revue Apologétique* (1929), pp. 5-26 and 129-145. *The Hypostatic Union and Created Actuation by the Uncreated Act* (West Baden, West Baden Press, Indiana), contains de la Taille's most important articles on this subject. See G. de Broglie's use of this concept in his *De Gratia,* cours polycopié (Paris, 1951), pp. 123-257.

5. D. Petavius, *Theologia Dogmatica* (Venice, Poleti, 1745), VIII, 5.

6. L. Thomassinus, *Dogmatica Theologica* (Paris, Ecalle, 1864-1872), VI, 2.

7. De Bovis, *op. cit.,* pp. 97-103; also de Broglie, *op. cit.,* pp. 123-126.

10

THE MODE OF GOD'S INDWELLING
(II)

FURTHER PROOF that the soul is actuated by the Uncreated Act is implicit in the concept of grace as the beginning of the beatific vision. From the union of the divine essence with the intelligence of the blessed soul there arises a genuine actuation of the human intelligence by the divine essence. Every type of knowledge within our experience implies by its nature some kind of immanence of the object to the subject. For instance, a man's knowledge of an apple involves the fact that the apple is somehow immanent to his mind, joined to his intelligence, not with its physical reality but in the intentional order of being—that is, as an idea. In other words, all knowledge implies some identification of the subject and the object, and this includes our knowledge in the beatific vision. In order that this vision may occur, God must somehow become immanent to the subject in a process of identification with it, not according to that form by which He subsists in Himself but according to an intentional, spiritual, intellectual form by means of which man's intelligence opens itself to the possession of the real. God is at once the term and object of the vision and its principle, inasmuch as He takes the place of the impressed image—the idea—in the intellect. But the divine act, the uncreated essence of God, in actuating our intelligence, never for a moment ceases to be divine, nor does it deprive our human nature of its own existence.

As we have noted earlier, God also actuates the human nature of Christ, but He does so by depriving the human nature of Christ of the connatural act of existence it would normally have as its own and substituting for it the act of existence of the Word. In this way God obliterates the human personality which would have possessed the human nature of Christ, had that nature received its own connatural act of existence. Since Christ's human nature does not have a created, proper act of existence, He is not a human person.

In the foregoing chapters we have taken care to stress that the state of grace is the ontological inchoation—the beginning, the seed, the first fruits—of the state of glory. Hence, even the baptized infant, independently of any meritorious acts, has the objective, ontological inchoation of the beatific vision. The newly baptized infant soul is therefore actuated by God, for the beatific vision is precisely this actuation of the intellect. The grace of the baptized infant is then an anticipation of the state of glory, a dynamism toward glory. The infant is already mobilized towards the beatific vision, interiorly energized towards it as a term. Possessing grace, the germ of the vision, the infant possesses in germ the actuation which the vision implies.

Charity and Faith

This actuation exists in the will of the infant, because it is by his will that he is moved towards his end. The will, thus energized in relation to its term, will achieve the beatific vision through its free activity.

There is also an actuation in the intellect of man, if we consider the intellect as an appetite for truth. Since it has as its final object total truth, and desires to possess this truth by complete knowledge, there is in man's intellect a rational appetite, an inchoation of actuation through the habit of faith, the obscure light of God's presence.

However, the actuation of the will by God presupposes in human wills a created perfection, a predisposition to actuation by God, for as we have said repeatedly, if there is to be a union of two things previously not united, there must be a change in one or in both. Since there can be no change in God, the actuator, then a change must take place in the will if it is to be united to the divine. This created change, or perfection in the will, is known as the infused virtue of charity.

As we have noted, some theologians have thought that we could dispense with the infused, created virtue of charity and with created sanctifying grace, since the Holy Spirit Himself suffices to enable man to place meritorious acts and disposes him for the beatific vision. This was the error, in particular, of Peter Lombard. But as we demonstrated in the last chapter, it is metaphysically impossible to conceive of an Uncreated Gift coming to the soul, or to the will or to the intellect, unless the soul or will or intellect is prepared for its reception. The Holy Spirit requires as a condition for His presence that the will be disposed to such possession, not because there is any insufficiency in the Holy Spirit but because conditions of union involve a change, and the Holy Spirit cannot Himself change. An actuation of intelligence or of will supposes that the intelligence or the will receives the Uncreated Act. But the act, in order to communicate itself to the potency, must change the receiver or dispose it, adapting it to its reception.

In the beatific vision God Himself adapts man's mind, adjusts it through the use of a creature which we call the light of glory. Through this adaptation the mind, altered by this creature, is able to receive God. No one, of course, save God, can actuate man or habilitate him to see the infinite. In the actuation of man's intelligence by faith, there are God, the intelligence, and faith, which is the actuation of man's intelligence by the Uncreated Act, God. In the will there are God, will, and the habit of charity, which is the created actuation in the will by the Uncreated Act, God. In grace there are God, the soul, and the created actuation which is sanctifying grace in the soul. This created actuation is, as we have emphasized, neither God nor man but a creature like other creatures, which is caused by the communication, the actuation, the self-donation of God to the soul.

By charity man is strengthened, empowered to seek God above all things and to prefer God before himself and other creatures. Charity impels man towards his final end, moving him towards the supreme good, helping to free him from the bonds of egotism. For the will to be so elevated there is needed a previous actuation of the soul's whole substance. Man acts through his intellect and through his will; he is the subject in whom are rooted these two powers, and it is he who chooses and thinks. Since action follows upon existence, if man is to act through his intellectual will it is proper that his soul, the fountainhead of these two faculties, should be elevated prior to the faculties. For if the act of will or intellect is to belong most fully to man, it should come from that which makes man most fully what he is, the soul itself.

It is undeniable that God could elevate one of man's faculties without elevating his soul. For instance, when man is in mortal sin but his sin is not against faith, he still retains faith, but although his intelligence is actuated by God, his soul is not. This is an abnormal situation, however, for the act of faith of one in mortal sin is in a certain sense posited at the fringe of the personality. The sinner, as man, is not fully committed to God; only his intellect is aligned with Him. The act of faith of one who is without love of God is not formed in charity. But if man makes a full commitment of himself to God in faith, he will live by faith and return to the state of charity.

To return to our discussion of the will of the baptized infant, we say that since its will is actuated its soul too must be actuated, and this actuation we call sanctifying grace. Flowing from a soul equally actuated, the will's actuation should be such as enables the will to grasp the Uncreated Object, God Himself. But this calls for a created actuation in the soul through the self-communication of the Uncreated Good Himself. In other words, the actuation is the Uncreated Good possessed in a created way.

Actuation of the Soul

Doubtless there are difficulties inherent in this theory of the actuation of the soul by God. Certain authors, for instance, restrict God's actuation to the faculties of the soul, the intellect and the will, since they do not see how it is possible for the soul itself to be actuated. It is their belief that the only conceivable actuation of the soul is of the essence-existence pattern; otherwise God would be replacing the proper act of existence of the soul by His own act of existence. We have already discussed this difficulty in the foregoing pages. Metaphysically speaking, all admit, this is possible, but as we have seen, if it occurred man would be hypostatically united to God and would have lost his own created personality.

The difficulty seems to dissolve, however, when we consider that the function of the act of existence is twofold: first, existence makes a person exist in himself, so that he cannot become a part of another; causes him to be this man closed off from anyone else. The second function of the act of existence (and it is this which God would supply in actuating the soul) constitutes the essence as the fountainhead whence flow one's potencies of intellect and will. For the essence is unable to exercise intellect and will until it receives its act of existence. As man's created act of existence gives to his essence the power to cause the emanation of an intellect and a will, so God, by His actuation, enables the soul to produce the supernatural faculties, the habits of faith and of charity. God does not become substantially united to man in the way man's essence is united to existence, but God unites Himself to man as a principle of operation enabling man's soul to pour out faith and charity.

In His actuation of man by grace God takes man as a completely constituted person, completely empowered already to exercise intellect and will in the natural order, and enables him to exercise a *supernatural* intelligence—faith—and a *supernatural* freedom—charity.

The objection brought against the theory of de la Taille, which we are espousing, is that it makes man substantially identified with God. But this is not so. Man has one substantial act of existence, a natural one, and in no sense does God take its place. But God does fulfill in a parallel fashion another function of the substantial act of existence; He enables the essence to exercise the supernatural habits, the supernatural faculties. We do not, then, have to limit the actuation of God to the faculties, and we can accept an actuation of the soul as long as it does not replace the created act of existence but fulfills in a higher and supernatural order one of its functions.

The Council of Trent, as we again recall, has said that there is only one formal cause of justification and that is *created grace*. We may not hold, then, as we have seen, that God is a formal cause but only that He is a quasi-formal cause. God does not, properly speaking, inform the soul or become a part of a superior composite made up of Himself and the soul. He actuates the soul without informing it; that is to say, in donating Himself He produces by quasi-formal causality the created actuation (sanctifying grace). And it is this which, properly speaking, informs the soul. God is joined to man by this self-donation; but He is not joined to the soul in a union of potency to act. The potency is the soul and the actuation is grace; the two are united and their union makes present the Act who is actuating; but the Act who is actuating does not inform the soul.

Is it possible to have an act which is not a form? Can one have an actuator who does not inform? It would seem so, for a valid explanation of the inhabitation demands that we posit something like an actuator who does not inform. There would have been no suspicion of the possibility of such an actuation were it not for revelation, but once revelation has posed this problem we may maintain the existence of an act which is not an inherent form. One cannot show that this is impossible; on the contrary, it seems to be highly probable.

One might call God the quasi-formal cause of the soul. By "quasi" we intend to exclude all the imperfections which generally belong to formal causes as we find them among creatures. The ordinary form becomes a part of the composite, but God cannot be a part of anything. The ordinary form is inferior in its perfection to the whole of which it is a composing part. This, of course, is not true of God. The ordinary form is limited by the potency which it informs. God is not limited by any potency but acts as a formal cause which has none of the imperfections we know in created formal causes.

A Transcendental Relation to God

Grace as a creature is the product of efficient causality. It is also a quasi-material cause because it is, as we have seen, a disposition preparing for the Act of God, and every disposition is in the order of material causality. Grace is also a formal cause, intrinsic and inherent. It inheres as an accident, a form, in the soul. And grace is the quasi-formal effect of a quasi-formal cause, God Himself. Hence there is a special union between the soul and God, not merely the union which is had when God produces an effect. Between sanctifying grace and the Uncreated Gift there is the closest possible nexus. We are dealing here with an intimate, metaphysical solidarity, for grace is the formal effect of the Giver, God; and grace is the ultimate disposition to the form, which is always produced by the form itself. Form cannot enter until the matter is prepared; matter cannot be fully prepared until the form begins to enter. Hence if sanctifying grace is the ultimate disposition for receiving God,

then there must be so close a unity between the two that they cannot possibly be separated. Sanctifying grace will be the last preparation made by the form.

The question is asked by some theologians: "How would one be
deified if he had sanctifying grace but did not have the Uncreated
Gift, the inhabitation?" The answer, as will be clear from all we
have said, is that the two are inseparable, one demands the other.

Everything about grace refers to God. In its ultimate analysis it is
a relation to God of the type which we call transcendental. That
is to say, grace is an absolute entity, although it may cause a relation. Grace is an absolute entity which by its whole being calls for
a relationship to another. This is what is meant by a transcendental
relation. Man's soul and body are absolute beings, but man's body
bears a relationship to his soul. It is the body *of* man's soul. After
death the soul keeps the transcendental relationship to the body,
because in its whole entity, in its whole being, it calls for a relationship to the body.

Ultimately, then, we could define grace as an absolute quality
which is a transcendental relationship to God actuating us. Such a
theory of actuation is not simply a metaphysical complication but
an explanation in metaphysical terms of the teaching of the Greek
Fathers and of St. Paul. To say that God is present as an act is to
say that we are introduced into His presence. He enriches us by
giving us Himself. Because we are rich with His divinizing power,
we are able to obtain from Him whatever we need.

Other Theories

It might be well at this point to speak of certain other theories
of the inhabitation which we consider insufficient to explain the
problem of the presence in us of the substance of God in a specifically new way.

The first theory is that of the theologian Vasquez, who explains the inhabitation by appealing to efficient causality, maintaining that God is present to the soul as an efficient cause, producing grace. The difficulty with this explanation is that it seems to effect only an intensification of the ordinary presence of immensity. Vasquez would reply that grace is such an extraordinary being that it must bring God's presence in an extraordinary fashion.[1] Actually, it seems to us, grace is such an extraordinary being precisely because it is not produced simply by efficient causality, but by quasi-formal causality. Grace is a share in the nature of God, because every formal cause donates or shares its own specific type of perfection. But this is not the function of an efficient cause. If a man makes a chair, the chair cannot think and choose or partake of the man's specific perfections. But if an intellectual soul acts as a formal cause to the body, then it follows that man can think because a formal cause shares its specific perfection with that which it informs.

Other theologians hold that the new presence is explained by the fact that grace is such a unique entity that in its production efficient causality and exemplary causality work so closely as to be almost identical. The exemplar, of which grace is an imitation, is of course the essence of God. But exemplary causality *always* works very closely with efficient causality. Moreover, this theory does not satisfy because it fails to explain the mystery of grace. It cannot explain how a creature, grace, produces a share in the *divine* nature in man. If grace were produced, as are all other creatures, by efficient causality alone, grace could not and would not make man a sharer in the divine nature, it seems to us. But if grace were produced by the impact of God giving Himself somewhat as a formal cause gives itself, then grace could not but give man a share in His perfection, because this is precisely the property of a formal cause. If God were to do this to the soul, were He to act as a form giving Himself to the soul, the effect would naturally be the kind of being we call sanctifying grace. It would be a sharing of nature. Exemplary causality, on the other hand, is always an idea in the mind of the cause. To join this with efficient causality does not improve the theory of efficient causality greatly.

Suarez maintains what is called the theory of the "objective presence." His explanation is that grace makes us friends of God, and since friendship either finds presence or creates it, God is newly present to the soul. But our answer to this is that though friendship may desire the presence of the friend it does not always succeed in producing it. Friends can be absent. Suarez would perhaps reply: "God can achieve a permanent presence to His friends." But this would simply be a reassertion of the problem. The theory of Suarez therefore is based upon friendship, but does not explain *how* the substance of God becomes newly present. Because one loves God and thinks of Him often, this does not make the substance of God present; it makes present an idea of God. But we must avoid reducing the inhabitation to an ideal or an intentional presence. It is the very being, the plenary reality of God Himself, that is present in a new way. Vasquez arrived at the concept of a substantial presence because he based his reasoning on the theory of efficient causality. But as we have seen, the presence he thus defined, although it was substantial, was not new. The presence Suarez defines is new, but is only a new thought; it is not substantial.[2]

The third theory is favored by most Thomists today. John of St. Thomas, one of the greatest commentators on the Angelic Doctor, held a theory which tries to combine the advantages of that of Vasquez and of Suarez with one new principle: quasi-experiential knowledge. In brief, the theory holds that God is always substantially present to the just soul by the ordinary presence of immensity. The substance of God is made present when He causes the soul to exist. However, when the just soul thinks about God, he comes into contact, in a quasi-experiential manner, with God already present in him.

In other words, the just soul has a quasi-experiential presence; he experiences God's presence within him by the presence of immensity.[3] Just as man's soul is present to him, and in his reflections upon his own acts, choices and thoughts, man achieves a sort of experiential knowledge of his soul, so in a somewhat similar way, when the soul in sanctifying grace acts, when it reflects upon God present within it, it becomes conscious of God as principle of its supernatural life; thus it has an experience of God present. God is newly present in the sense that He is now present as an object known, and an object loved, experientially.

There are, however, difficulties in this theory. A sinner has God substantially present by the presence of immensity. If a sinner thinks of God and even makes an act of faith in God, according to this theory, it seems, he should possess the inhabitation. John of St. Thomas would doubtless reply: the sinner's knowledge of God and his contact with Him will not be quasi-experiential; it will not be an experience of God, because God is not dwelling in the sinner. But would He not be there actually present in His substance by the presence of immensity? Again we can imagine John of St. Thomas replying that one can come into contact with, or experience, God only if He is present by grace. But many in grace insist that they have never had this quasi-experience of God; are we then to be deprived of the inhabitation because we are not mystics? Revelation does not limit the inhabitation to these chosen few.

Moreover, the baptized infant possesses the indwelling God (the inhabitation), and the infant does not think at all, much less have mystical experiences. Man possesses God when he sleeps, and he is not then thinking or having mystical experiences. The tepid, the slovenly, the lazy have the inhabitation, as do those who commit multitudes of venial sins, and they are not ordinarily granted the grace of the experiential presence of God. We cannot subscribe to a theory which excludes the infant, the lazy, the dull, the unfervent, and the non-mystical from the inhabitation. Some maintain that although the infant does not have the experience of God he has the *power* to experience God. To this we object that what the infant has now would be only a potential inhabitation, not one which is actual.

Revelation, however, makes it clear that the infant actually has the inhabitation from the moment of baptism.

Summary

Since one cannot easily accept any of these theories, and we have excluded other possibilities, we return to the theory of Father de la Taille, based upon the probable presumption that an uncreated formal cause will have none of the imperfections of the created formal cause. It is true that we can neither prove nor disprove this because we have no experience of an uncreated formal cause. But if the theory is acceptable, it gives a very clear explanation of God's substantial presence in a new way to the soul in grace and to no one else. And it also explains clearly why grace produces its marvellous effects in the soul. For if grace is the self-donation of God, then it is obvious that grace will produce a share in the divine nature, because the function of a formal cause is to give of its own perfection to the potency. Moreover, the theory unifies the whole tract on grace, for it explains all the formal effects of grace. By sanctifying grace one is made a friend of God, and friendship implies some kind of equality of nature. If God wishes to call a man a friend, He must divinize his nature; if man is to act on the level of friendship with God, he must have a share in His nature. If the theory is correct, God, donating Himself, would do what every formal cause does: He would give of His specific perfection, His proper intellectuality and spirituality. Man would then be raised to a quasi-equality with Him, a quasi-equality of nature, and could act as a friend. It is obvious also that if the theory is true, grace would expel sin from the soul, for grace would be nothing but the communication of God Himself to the soul.

Finally it is clear that man can be referred to as a child of God, for a child has the same nature as the parents. If grace is produced by formal causality, man will truly be a child of God, for in giving to him a share in His own nature, God would bring man into His divine family.

NOTES

1. *Opera* (Lyons, Gardan, 1631), *In I,* q. 8, a. 3. J. Terrien, *La Grâce et la Gloire* (Paris, Lethielleux, 1901), holds much the same position.

2. *Opera* (Paris, Vives, 1854), *De Trinitate,* L. XII, I, I, c. V., n. 10-13.

3. John of St. Thomas, *Cursus Theologicus* (Solesmes, 1934-1936), *De Trinitate,* q. 43, d. 37, a. 3.

11

OUR RELATIONSHIP TO
FATHER, SON AND
HOLY SPIRIT

THE PROBLEM to be discussed in this chapter is that of the special
and distinct relationship of grace to each of the three divine Persons.
At first sight it might seem as if no such relationship existed, since
every work that God accomplishes outside the Trinity is common
to all three Persons. Thus, for example, the production of that
created grace which justifies man is brought about by all three
Persons. Moreover, it seems impossible to conceive of a relationship
between man and a single Person of the Trinity which would not
be hypostatic or substantial, that is, a union of the type that obtains
between the human nature of Christ and His divine nature. Yet
Sacred Scripture and Tradition at least suggest the possibility of
distinct relationships to each Person of the Trinity, intimating that
man is united to the divinity not only as common to the three
Persons, but also as possessed in a distinct and incommunicable
manner by each divine Person.[1]

The Father holds the divine essence under the relationship of
paternity, the Son under the relationship of filiation, and the Holy
Spirit as passive spiration. Thus, the Son proceeds from the non-
proceeding Father, the Principle without principle, by way of
intellection, the Son being the Word, the total, substantial and
never-to-be-repeated image of the Father. All further processions by

way of intellect are excluded, since the Word is infinite. To find a third Person in the Trinity, one must look to another mode of procession, that by way of the will. The will of the Father and that of the Son, as one principle, breathe forth actively their love, and this love, as breathed forth passively, is the Holy Spirit.

Each Person of the Trinity possesses the divine essence and all that is common to it without differentiation of degree or temporal sequence, but in a distinct, incommunicable and personal manner, somewhat as each angle, in a distinct way, dominates the entire surface of the triangle. The sole distinction among the Persons is that based upon relative opposition: one Person is not another. Our question, then, is: is man united to the divine existence inasmuch as it is common to all three Persons, or insofar as it is possessed by each? Has man, in grace, a distinct relation to each Person of the Trinity? Does each exercise a distinct function in our sanctification?

We know from Scripture that the Father has adopted man; from His name is derived all paternity in heaven and on earth (Ephes. 3:15). This adoptive sonship is an image of the unique sonship of the Word, who is the first born of many brothers (Rom. 8:29). Christ, the Word, is the exemplary and meritorious cause of man's sonship, but it is the Father who is its principle. The Holy Spirit is the principle in whom God confers the sonship; the Father imitates the sonship of the Word and confers this imitation upon the Christian through the Holy Spirit. Scripture repeatedly insists that the Holy Spirit is the One who indwells. There is, however, the possibility we have already touched upon, that both man's sanctification and the indwelling are assigned to the Holy Spirit only by appropriation.

Special Mode of Our Sonship

The Fathers always speak of the Christian as a son of the Father, which would seem to indicate that we are related to Him in a special way as His sons, for we are never called sons of the Word or of the Holy Spirit. The liturgy of the Church is in accord with the practice of the Fathers, for in it we are always referred to as Sons of God or of the Father. Our sonship, moreover, is described as an imitation of the sonship of the eternal Word, and certainly His sonship is referred directly and exclusively to God the Father, not to God the Son or to God the Holy Spirit. Although the Fathers are fully aware of the fact that God's operation outside the Trinity is always common to all three Persons, they still explain our adoption as an adoption "by the Father, through the Son, in the Holy Spirit." It seems as if we could grant to the Father some role in our sonship which relates us especially to Him as its author, and that consequently the eternal Father is the source of our divine sonship in a special fashion not shared by the Son or the Holy Spirit.[2]

Moreover, as we have seen, our sonship is a participation in the eternal sonship of the Word. We are brothers of the second Person of the Trinity, and hence some special relationship to Him may be suggested. Then, too, Scripture indicates for the Holy Spirit a role in our sanctification that is particularly unitive, which perhaps suggests a special relationship of man to the Holy Spirit also. To the Fathers, the Holy Spirit is the substantial bond of personal union within the Trinity, and the bond that unites man to God. Our union is always *to* the Father, *through* Christ, *in* the Holy Spirit. The Holy Spirit seems actively to maintain in the life of man's sanctification a role parallel to the one He fulfills in the Trinity. It would appear reasonable also to suppose that the third Person might achieve a union with man by which he would be united to the Trinitarian life, thus becoming for man the bond of union to God with a special relationship to Himself.

Scripture and tradition suggest this, but the idea is in apparent conflict with the long-accepted assertion that all works *ad extra* are common to the three Persons. The Fathers affirm that wherever there is *efficient* causality outside the Trinity all three Persons act, the magisterium of the Church constantly asserts it, and St. Thomas, along with many other philosophers and theologians, stresses the same axiom. Consequently it would seem that we must abandon the idea that we are sons of the Father and admit that we are sons of the entire Trinity.

Sanctifying grace as a created gift is produced in man by the three Persons acting through one divine nature. *Under this aspect*, of course, grace cannot introduce man into a special relationship with any one Person. But there is another aspect under which this can happen, for sanctifying grace is an entity of union, as Emile Mersch has so beautifully put it. Sanctifying grace, as we have constantly reiterated, is essentially related to the Uncreated Gift and cannot exist in man without the presence of the Uncreated Being. Through sanctifying grace the three Persons communicate themselves to man's soul. No proper relationship can come through *efficient* causality because no one of the three Persons can exert this causality without the other two. But since grace is also a being of union, it may produce a special relationship of *union* to each Person of the Trinity. For although produced by the three in common, it could imply an actuation of the soul by the Uncreated Act as this Uncreated Act is held in distinct, personal, and incommunicable fashion by the Father, the Son and the Holy Spirit. Consequently it seems possible to assert that the union of man and the Trinity could be immediate and in relation to each of the Persons.[3]

Here we must refer once more to a difficulty which we have encountered repeatedly in other connections. The foregoing theory seems to imply a substantial or hypostatic union of God and man, such that man becomes God, since in communicating Himself directly a divine Person can only give what is properly His own, which could only be His personality. So it might appear that this relationship could be created only by substituting for man's human personality His personal act of existence, by which He would make man a divine Person, like Christ. It is possible, however, in the present connection, to conceive of a union with the three Persons which would be accidental rather than substantial or hypostatic. For in the beatific vision the blessed see God face-to-face, not simply as one divine nature, but as three divine Persons. But this beatific vision is impossible without an antecedent union of the known object, the three divine Persons, with the knower, man. If man is to know the three Persons of the Blessed Trinity as Father, Son, and Holy Spirit, there must be a union of each person with man's mind in the beatific vision antecedent to man's knowledge of each Person. Although man can know a creature through its image, he cannot grasp God in any image, for every image is finite, whereas God is infinite. The only adequate image of God is the Word. Consequently, in the beatific vision man cannot have an image intervening between himself and God; the vision is immediate, direct, face-to-face. The three Persons must join themselves to man's mind antecedently to his knowledge of them, because they take the place in his mind of the image of normal intellection.

Hence, for man to know the three Persons as Persons, each must be united to man's mind as a Person prior to his knowledge of Him in a union somehow brought about by way of actuation. Now God is as a quasi-form in the beatific vision, actuating the intellect in the manner of a form or an idea, although He is by no means a form or an idea. We cannot, obviously, conceive this kind of actuation as being achieved through *efficient* casuality, but we can conceive of it as being accomplished through quasi-formal causality. This ontological communication, which the divine Persons make of themselves to the intelligence of the blessed to render the beatific vision possible, does not destroy man's created personality; yet we know that some kind of accidental information or actuation is achieved by each of the three divine Persons.

Is it possible that the three divine Persons unite themselves to the just man in somewhat the same way? Grace is the beginning of vision, and what is true of the vision ought to be true of its earthly principle, since sanctifying grace bears an essential relationship to the immediate ontological possession of the vision. Hence the fact of the beatific vision, wherein each divine Person unites Himself

to man's mind as a Person, suggests that something of the same kind
may be true of man in grace, and that man may possess a distinct
relationship to each of the three divine Persons.

Our Relationship to Christ's Humanity

Although the principal cause of grace in man is always the three
divine Persons, sanctifying grace being always a created element,
the instrument that produces it is Christ. Because it is He who has
merited grace for man, and because man imitates Him, grace comes
through His humanity. Thus it seems that one can say that man
has a relationship to Christ's humanity which he does not have to
the other two persons of the Trinity. We are speaking here of the
relationship to Christ as Man, not of a relationship to Christ as
God, the Word, the Second Person of the Trinity. The only proper
relationship of man to Christ as God, as far as we can see, is that in
which man imitates Christ's sonship. But it does not seem impossible
to maintain on the basis of this imitation that man has a proper
relationship to the Word, even as God.[4]

We cannot understand clearly how man can have a special relationship to the Word as Word, because the sanctifying action of the
Word is had in common with the Son and the Holy Spirit, and all
three Persons touch man through their common instrument, the
humanity of Christ. Perhaps one could say that man is specially
related to the divinity of the Word at least through His humanity.
But could one also say that the instrumental influence of Christ's
humanity is not only an efficient influence, but one that somehow also
includes an immediate union to the Person of the Son, a union
realized in the Holy Spirit? The Son possesses the divine existence
under the relationship of filiation in a way that is distinct, incommunicable and proper to Himself as Son, whereas the instrumental
influence of the humanity of Christ and the principal efficiency are
common to the whole divinity. It does seem possible to say that

there is a quasi-actuation, or an actuation by quasi-formal causality, similar to the actuation of the beatific vision. To know the divinity as Persons, man must be united to them, and this union can take place only if he is actuated by them. Man in grace is united to the Son, with the result that what is personal and proper to the Son is communicated to man by way of union or actuation. Once united to the Son, man would imitate His sonship, and therefore would have also a proper relationship of sonship to the Father. This would be accomplished in the Holy Spirit, the bond of love between the Father and the Son in heaven, who would also become the bond uniting man to the Son, thus making him the son of the Father, exerting a specific function in man's sanctification, and founding a distinct relationship to Himself.

NOTES

1. P. De Letter reviews many of the recent articles on this subject in "Sanctifying Grace and the Divine Indwelling," *Theological Studies* (1953), pp. pp. 242-272.

2. Bourassa, "Rôle personnel des personnes et relations distinctes aux personnes," *Sciences Ecclésiastiques* (1955), p. 152 ff.

3. See M. Donnelly, "Inhabitation of the Holy Spirit," *Proceedings of the American Catholic Theological Society* (1949), pp. 39-77.

4. See de Bovis, *op. cit.*, pp. 116-127.

12

MERIT: FACT AND THEORY

WE HAVE STUDIED at length the effect of grace with regard to the existence of man; we shall now discuss its effect upon his activity. The value attached to the actions of the just man is termed merit—a word that evokes a certain malaise among many Christians. The idea that the imperfect activity of a creature could be such as to enable him to claim certain *rights* to divine goods makes them feel uneasy. The capacity of man to win heaven, not only as an inheritance but as a reward to which he is entitled in justice, seems too great an exaltation of human personality. Man can perceive without very much difficulty that his evil acts are worthy of punishment, even in strictest justice. But that divine goods are due to him in justice seems odd indeed. That he can merit well of men, deserve rewards in justice from them, may be evident, but it is not so easy to grasp the fact that before God, to whom he owes his being and life, and absolute obedience, he may be equally deserving of rewards in justice. Yet it is certain that the power to merit, to deserve rewards, is one of the consequences of man's supernatural dignity and is graciously willed by God.

Human acts can have a value marking them as worthy of a reward from God. All that we have and are we owe to Him. If this is so in the order of nature, it is even more so in the supernatural order, which is absolutely gratuitous, for God's sovereign independence and absolute dominion require it. It is with no abdication of His limitless rule that He graciously binds Himself to reward our good actions. In doing so He rewards His own goodness, for the source of all merit is His gift of grace. He has chosen to become our debtor by promising a reward for our good deeds. It is only His promise to reward us that enables us to claim a reward.

That He has attached a reward in justice to our good acts is clear from revelation, as we shall see. Nor does it in any way detract from the greatness of Christ's redemption to claim that man merits heaven by his works. For Christ is the one who merited for us that grace out of which comes our merit. He is the root, the source of all our graces, since He obtained for us the power to merit and the gracious promise of God to reward our good deeds. Man's merit rests upon two absolutely gratuitous gifts of God: His promise to reward and the first infusion of sanctifying grace, both of which come to us wholly from the divine liberality and initiative.

Merit is a quality of a free act which incurs a moral debt. Since a good work done in homage to another is worthy of a reward, the basis of merit is found to be in justice. Thus it differs from prayer, which appeals to the kindness and liberality of God, and from satisfaction, which appeals through reparation of an injury.

Condign Merit

Our discussion will deal chiefly with *condign* merit—i.e., merit to which a reward is due in justice. There is another kind of merit which theologians term *congruous*, but it is merit in a less strict sense because it appeals to equity or generosity rather than to justice.

This, of course, is a juridical framework, employed in accordance with tradition and for the sake of clarity. However, when we deal with the intense interpersonal dialogue between God and the individual Christian, we may complement the juridical framework with one which is psychological.

The references to merit in Sacred Scripture must be interpreted in the light of the truth that grace and glory are continuous. Man is divinized in his being and hence is divinized in his activity, and the life of grace issues in the life of heaven. A proof which emphasizes the notion of justice in merit can be found in the scriptural use of words like "reward." "Rejoice and exult, because your reward is great in heaven" (Matt. 5:12). "The fire will assay the quality of everyone's work: if his work abides which he has built thereon, he will receive reward . . ." (1 Cor. 3:13-14). Also such words as "prize" and "crown" suggest merit. "But one thing I do: forgetting what is behind, I strain forward to what is before, I press on towards the goal, to the prize of God's heavenly call in Christ Jesus" (Phil. 3:13-14). "Do you not know that those who run in a race, all indeed run, but one receives the prize? So run as to obtain it. And everyone in a contest abstains from all things—and they indeed to receive a perishable crown, but we an imperishable" (1 Cor. 9:24-25). The crown mentioned in the test, however, is not given *out of* justice, but *from* justice—that is, it is the organic fulfillment of sanctifying grace. Moreover, it is bestowed by a *just* judge: "I have fought the good fight, I have finished the course, I have kept the faith. For the rest, there is laid up for me a crown of justice, which the Lord, the just Judge, will give to me in that day" (2 Tim. 4:7-8). Since the giver is a *just* judge, it is intimated that the crown is merited in justice. So too, in the Epistle to the Colossians: "Whatever you do, work at it from the heart as for the Lord and not for men, knowing that from the Lord you will receive the inheritance as your reward" (Col. 3:23-24). Man, therefore, has some rights with God acquired through good works.

The Fathers teach merit so clearly that even the Protestants *admit* that the Fathers teach it. Besides the figure of the crown won in the stadium by striving and effort, the Fathers use the idea of military pay. Presumably the soldier worked for his pay and earned it in justice. They appeal also to the scale of just balance, and to the divine promises. Cyprian uses the word merit, and the Latin Fathers are particularly devoted to metaphors taken from commutative jus-

tice (the strictest form of justice) and even from commercial trans-
actions.

Great care must be exercised in discussing the nature of merit
in title of justice. In human relations when two people are equal,
the concept of merit evokes the idea of strict justice or right, exact
retribution. In such human merit, the juridical character of contract
is predominant: a man does so much and receives so much reward.
But in the case of a human and divine relationship there is the
obvious difficulty that man is not the equal of God, and furthermore
that man owes everything to God. Since we can in no way equate
human with divine merit, it is almost necessary to forget the juridical
origin of the term.

De la Taille's Theory

According to de la Taille's theory, which we have set forth in
the preceding pages, man somehow seizes the very riches and
power of God Himself through the divine inhabitation. When we
consider the acts of the just man as they proceed from God within
him, it is possible to speak of a strict merit, a strict proportion. Again,
although man merits because he collaborates with God by his free
will, the primacy always rests with God, the first cause. Now God,
as the cause of merit, has obviously a perfect arithmetical proportion
to God, the term of merit, since there is absolute equality between
the two. Since it is God Himself within man who lends him the
ability to proportion his activity to eternal life, it follows that
under this aspect supernatural merit is even more rigorously just
than is natural merit.[1]

Considered under another aspect, the application of the notion of
human merit to our supernatural relationships is an analogical
process. The analogy involved is restrictive, of course, for supernatural merit cannot be as rigorously just. Man may have the perfection of justice and merit only when the two persons involved are

absolutely equal; but even among men such perfect equality does not often exist. Between a servant and a master, between a pupil and his teacher, between a child and his father, one can hardly speak of strict justice, because there is not strict equality. Since everything we have is a gift of God, we cannot speak of merit according to the strictest terms of justice.

When God has given Himself and grace, then grace demands by its very nature that it fulfill itself in heaven. Barring man's resistance, it is unthinkable that God would refuse to accomplish what is inscribed in the very nature of grace. For as we have seen in other connections, the relationship of grace to glory is not simply a juridical one, nor is the beatific vision a reward exterior to grace. The reward of the meritorious act is inscribed in the act itself and in the principle of the act—which is grace. Merit is really a divine ordination, interior to the reality of grace itself, a real beginning of heaven.

We must remember also that the right to eternal glory always remains conditioned in the just man. He does not merit the conservation of the title to glory. As long as he is in the state of sanctifying grace he has a right to heaven, but he has no strict right to remain in the state of sanctifying grace. He may fall from it by sin. Especially, man has no right to the final grace of perseverance, but must ask for it; if he asks with perseverance, God will give it infallibly, because He has so promised, yet one cannot ask unless His grace inspires within one the desire to ask; so, again, the initiative is God's.

The Church therefore has recognized in the works of the just man a title in justice, but not to the extent that man may boast of his goodness or speak of his rights before God. While admitting that we have a dignity and a value in our good works, the Church insists that the very principle of merit is a gift continually given to us from a loving God.

Merit is possible because grace is a mysterious appropriation of the power of the Holy Spirit, and this power always remains divine. Grace is not merely something man works with; it is always the gift of a person, and it always retains its character of gift. It is our fearful poverty and the immense mercy and goodness of God that should be emphasized in discussing merit, not the puerile conception according to which grace is a kind of magic which man employs to acquire rights from the divinity. What man is engaged in is an interpersonal drama, and therefore we must explore its ontology and its psychology.

What are the conditions for merit? First of all, one must be living and in the state of grace, since grace is the root of merit. Man needs the state of grace to merit strictly, for only in that state is he deified, a son of God and in the state of friendship with God. The meritoriousness of the deed is largely proportioned to the degree of likeness to God in the agent—in other words, to the degree of sanctifying grace he possesses. If man clings to grave sin, his act cannot be orientated towards God in such a way as to merit a reward in justice. To be heirs we must also be sons. Actual grace does not create a proportion between the work done and the reward in justice because acts done only from actual grace do not spring from a source divinized in its principle. The sinner who avails himself of actual grace may yet remain a sinner, deprived of the divine dignity, the godlike quality of a child of God. While actual grace suffices to fulfill the requirements for merit in equity, it is insufficient for merit in justice. The souls in purgatory are excluded from meriting, for both Scripture and tradition seem to say that there is, by divine decree, no meriting beyond the doors of death. Secondly, freedom of choice is required, free coöperation with God. One must be able to choose this act or that act, or at least be able to choose to act or not to act. Thirdly, the work performed must be virtuous. Fourthly, while we do not demand of man an intention so actual and explicit as to say, with each act, "I want to merit," he must have in the concrete a virtual and implicit intention of wanting to merit. This is had by every Christian who is ordained to God through sanctifying grace, since such a man not only is, but presumably wants to be, so ordained and to act accordingly. Consequently no good act of man is sterile towards eternal life because of a lack of intention unless the intention has been withdrawn. However, man should renew his intention from day to day and not allow his baptismal intentions to be the only ones to reign in his soul. The good works of a man in the state of grace need only conform to the divine law. His actions are then orientated to God, for the total giving of himself to God by the state of grace subsists as long as mortal sin has not made him retract this orientation. Once given to God by grace, all man's good acts are drawn to God by the fundamental movement of love that is habitual charity.

Eternal Life as an Object of Merit

Considering now the objects of merit we ask: is the eternal life of glory an object of merit? Man really merits eternal glory but, paradoxically, his actual achievement of glory is contingent on the gift of final perseverance, which he cannot merit. Accidental glory is certainly an object of condign merit, as are the increase of accidental glory, the glorification of the body, the society of the angels and of the blessed. An increase of glory is obviously an object of condign merit because it is parallel to an increase in sanctifying grace itself.

Actual graces, too, are objects of condign merit, at least insofar as they give man the power to persevere. This is logical, for man needs actual grace to preserve sanctifying grace, to avoid sin and to overcome the temptations that threaten his life of grace. Moreover, the state of grace is fundamentally a life, and a life-principle would not be adequate if it did not possess the capacity to grow and express itself in action as well as to defend itself against what would destroy it. Hence it is normal that one who possesses sanctifying grace should be able to merit in justice the graces needed for progress in life, the defense of life and the expansion of its energies.

He can merit all that he needs to persevere in the state of grace. And we know that one can obtain actual perseverance also by prayer.

Congruous Merit

Congruous merit is quite different from the merit we have discussed so far. It is based upon a title which appeals to the liberality or generosity of the giver, or to his sense of equity or fairness, and it is only called merit by analogy. It was not distinguished from condign merit until the thirteenth century. Congruous and condign merit are not two species of the same genus. Since congruous merit suppresses the relationship of justice founded on strict rights, it cannot strictly be defined as merit at all. Neither the Church nor the common consent of theologians imposes this concept upon us, and in fact for certain authors the notion of congruous merit is extremely vague and unsubstantiated. We believe, however, that it should be retained because of the light it throws on the doctrine of the Communion of Saints. The just man, in sanctifying grace, cannot merit condignly for another, but he can merit congruously for another all that he can merit condignly for himself. If we are to reject this idea of congruous merit for others in the Mystical Body, we are left with only the notion of impetration and satisfaction. But since this would seem to impoverish the relationships that exist in the Mystical Body, we believe that the doctrine of congruous merit must find a place here also.

The Christian in sanctifying grace can merit in equity—that is, congruously—for others such things as the grace of conversion, of final perseverance and also the first actual grace leading to conversion. The reason for this power is the intimate friendship which sanctifying grace establishes between the just man and God; hence the traditional prayers of the Church for the conversion of the sinner and the strengthening of the people of God.

The Christian in the state of grace may probably merit for himself in equity future conversion from mortal sin if he should fall. One of the reasons for this is the plight of the sinner. The sinner disposing himself for justification cannot condignly merit because he does not have one of the conditions: sanctifying grace. Yet, with the aid of actual graces, he can merit further actual graces, thus congruously meriting his justification. There is a certain proportion between the goodness of his acts done with actual grace and a reward, although the proportion addresses itself not to justice but to the divine liberality. To the sinner who accepts the first grace, God promises a new grace, and this is infallible congruous merit. Infallible congruous merit is that which will *certainly* be given because God has bound Himself by His promise.

Fallible congruous merit is that which is *not certainly* given, because God has made no promise in its regard. One can merit final perseverance congruously, but only fallibly, because God has promised it as an answer to prayer, not good works. God has also said that He will give further graces to the sinner who accepts one grace.

A difficulty raised against the notion of congruous as distinguished from condign merit is that it involves an anthropomorphic concept of God. Although condign merit appeals to God's justice, and congruous merit to His fidelity, liberality, generosity, these are all identified in God, and therefore, say some, the distinction is absurd. But the distinction is not at all absurd, since although God's justice and fidelity are not really distinct *within Him,* their effects do resemble more closely one or another of the divine attributes. Thus one can say correctly that God expresses His justice in this action and His mercy in that. When God shows Himself kind to the prodigal son, although His justice is operating as much as His mercy, it is fitting that we speak of His mercy to the sinner. Consequently, we cannot disregard the distinction between the two attributes.

The objects of congruous merit will clearly be more extensive than those of merit in justice, since the conditions for congruous merit are not so rigorous, and congruous merit does not require *sanctifying* grace as its principle.

One may, for example, congruously merit the first infusion of sanctifying grace. One could not possibly merit that in justice, since, by definition, one lacks one of the conditions for merit in justice, namely sanctifying grace. One can also merit in equity, although not in justice, all the graces that lead up to the first infusion of sanctifying grace, with one exception: one cannot merit in any way the first actual grace, since one is utterly deprived of *any* principle of merit, either transitory or permanent. But by coöperation with one actual grace he merits in equity another. One can even, if he coöperates with a whole series of actual graces, congruously merit the first infusion of sanctifying grace. The reason one can merit justification thus is because all the previous good acts done with actual grace have a material finality which is ordained precisely to justification.

There is another question we might ask: can one in any sense merit efficacious graces—that is, graces which infallibly ensure man's free coöperation, and hence have an infallibly certain connection with the placing of the free virtuous act? Theologians commonly hold that one cannot merit efficacious graces in justice. One may indeed merit sufficient grace in justice—i.e., graces which give all the power required to place the good act but whose connection with the good act is not infallible. But theologians commonly deny that one can merit efficacious graces in justice, for if we could, we would be able to merit in justice final perseverance, which depends on efficacious grace. Having received gratuitously one's first efficacious grace and coöperated with it, one can congruously merit other efficacious graces; one cannot, however, condignly merit them. Even this congruous merit, moreover, is a *fallible* merit, because God has promised sufficient grace, He has not promised efficacious grace. One may also, as we have said, merit congruously, but fallibly, for another, all that he can merit condignly for himself, and probably also the first grace for another.

The sinner too can merit graces, even efficacious graces, but congruously only; he would always require an actual grace to merit another one.

Merit a Fruit

Christ is the true vine, we are the branches; if we remain united to Him we have the power to bear fruit. This is the meaning of merit. God communicates to us His grace and His love with which we can produce constantly more intense grace and love as the fruit of His initial gifts. They are certainly not the merits of our poor humanity alone but the merits of Christ communicating to us the freedom to say yes to His solicitations. Man can tend to eternal life, proportion his acts to eternal life and gain entrance to the fatherland—heaven. The Christian who remains in the love of Christ can merit an increase of love and the eternal presence of the Beloved. The recompense he seeks is not something strange or extrinsic to his love, but the face-to-face presence of the Beloved, the source and support of his love. No Christian love, no love worthy of the name, could fail to seek this reward. Love of its nature desires union. We shall see Him "as He is." As all love seeks reciprocity, the salvific love of Christ has empowered man to reply to His love. To Him belong the honor and the glory of all human merit, and in crowning our deeds with a reward, He crowns His own generosity. At eventide we shall be judged by love, but the very love we have given to Christ is itself a gift from Him, the source of all goodness.

Our conversation is already in heaven; we are fellow-citizens of the saints, members of God's household; the Christ is risen and we should seek the things that are above. How often the future tenses of the Old Testament have become present tenses in the New! The saving act of Christ has been objectively accomplished; something has already come to pass. We know that we have passed from death to life (1 John 3:14). We have eternal life (1 John 5:13). We have peace with God through Our Lord Jesus Christ (Rom. 5:1) and Christ lives in us. We dwell in Him and He in us, for He has given us of His Spirit (1 John 3:24). Our conformation to Christ demands a perpetual effort, but Christ has given us the means of attaining salvation. For by faith and baptism we are freed from the triple slavery to sin, to death and to the law, and we are now risen with Christ and seated with Him at the right hand of the Father. To those who adhere to Christ by faith and charity God shows Himself faithful, and nothing save sin itself can separate them from the charity of Christ. This Christian hope is the source of joy and peace to the faithful. The Holy Spirit prays within the Christian with ineffable groanings, and he is destined in a renewed creation to receive the reward of his merits, the full glorification of the sons of God, the final term of merit.

NOTES

1. See the applications of de la Taille's theory to the concept of merit in G. de Broglie, *De Gratia,* pp. 167-172. Cf. also de Bovis, *op. cit.,* p. 173.

13

CONCLUSION

THE DIVINE ACT which is grace is not something alien to the aspirations or the nature of man. While infinitely surpassing his nature, it works from within upon his interior, fulfilling his obscure dynamism to possess the triune God. From the first moment of history the fact of God's call to man to enter into supernatural intimacy with Him has wondrously affected his existential situation. The saving will of God operative in Christ has placed in man an implicit desire to transcend his nature and fulfill the fundamental aspirations of his personality through the acceptance of God's freely offered grace. The state of grace to which God invites man achieves a profound reorientation towards intimacy with the Trinity. It fosters an option in the very depths of man's existence of which he is obscurely, though never fully, conscious. The certitude of his filial orientation to God, though perceived more in action than in analysis, is lived. In the love of God and man to which grace solicits us, the Christian moves toward a dark knowledge of his own commitment to God and of God's gracious response.

The life of grace thus implies a dim sentiment of the divine presence which only in the mystics brightens to a genuine "experience" of God. This presence within man works slowly and organically, from the interior outward, bringing to calm maturity his sensibility and will. The gracious influence of God penetrates the center of man's existence, gradually forms all the regions of his humanity, and continually urges him to realize the full development of his powers through the total gift of his heart in filial love. By delivering man from fatal self-obsession, by involving him in a mysterious, personal encounter with Christ, it redirects his fundamental drives, desires and the liberty of his will.

With the growth of the life of grace the element of personal encounter becomes more prominent, leaving always, however, a breach between the consciousness of God and faith's apprehension of Him. In grace it is God Himself who comes to meet man, but the supernatural itself is not the immediate object of awareness. Still it is a meeting of persons, beyond the range of the purely conceptual, in the high knowledge that accompanies a free surrender in love. Man's obscure awareness of God discovers in Him someone who wills his good, who favors his interests, who invites a response of loving surrender. The action of God at Christian baptism evokes within man the capacity to respond to love with love. In the spirit, that center of personal density where one is most himself, the Christian is aware of a clear invitation to total acceptance of another in faith, hope and charity.

It is to the life of faith and love that grace invites us, and not to any moralism of "correctness." This demands not less but more abnegation of egotism than would a multitude of legal observances, but its invitation is to freedom. Christian liberty is a fruit of the faith and grace given at baptism and the perpetual effort to respond to the Christ. It is true liberty leading to eternal life, the new law which is not merely given us but is accomplished within us through the interior action of the Person of the Spirit. Receiving sanctifying grace at baptism, we receive the Spirit who becomes within us a principle of activity, aiding us to produce His fruits— joy, peace, patience, and all the Christian expressions of charity. In the measure in which we deepen our faith and love for the Christ whose grace we possess will the observance of His commandments appear as an inner demand of faith and love itself.

For the Christian consciously to further the dialogue between God and man, there is needed an awareness of the nature of grace as unitive being. It is a mistake to think of grace as a complete, independently existing entity instead of a being which arises in man because he is united to God and only because of this union. Grace is essentially orientated to God, the created effect of God's self-gift to man, and therefore never to be conceived as existing apart from the divinizing union of God with the soul. In His approach to man, God respects his nature while fulfilling it in a transcendent order. The plenitude of being itself, He is able to communicate Himself to man without destroying or even doing violence to human nature.

Grace, in each man, adapts itself to the individual lines of his personality, transfiguring his humanity, divinizing his unique individuality. At once thoroughly personal and social, it perfects man as he is, in a union with the supremely one yet triune God. The divinizing power of grace lies precisely in the fact that it is a unitive entity which attaches man to God in the mystery of His inner life, and opens the way to supernatural union with all men in Christ. By it man exists in a divine fashion, able to call God "Father" with a resonance impossible without grace; by it man possesses God not as an object upon which he seizes, but as one whose possession alters his whole mode of being, so intimate is the union. And by it man is restored to a plenary self-possession, becoming by grace more fully himself, existing in a new way, as a new creature re-created in the image of the one who divinizes him.

Because it comes to sinful beings, the grace of Christ is redemptive, adapted to heal the wounds of human nature. Provided only its dynamism is allowed to develop, it is able to transfigure erring humanity, connaturalizing man to the mode of existence proper to the first-born of many brothers, accomplishing his growth in the life of Christ until he is worthy to join the company of the elect in the victorious eschatological kingdom where struggle and defeat have no role, where grief will be unknown and God Himself will wipe away all tears. In the words of Clement of Alexandria: *"Baptisati illuminamur; illuminati in filios adoptamur; adoptati perficimur, perfecti immortales reddimur."* "Being baptized, we are enlightened; being enlightened, we are adopted into sonship; being adopted, we are made perfect; being perfected, we are rendered immortal."

APPENDICES

APPENDIX I

LUTHER AND REFORM

THE JUDGMENTS passed on Luther in the course of history have been so frequently partisan that it is almost impossible for the historian of today to arrive at anything like an objective study of his person. The Lutheran Church has revered him as a saint, a prophet, a wonder-worker. Radical Protestantism has seen him rather as a genius and a national hero. Romanticism has considered him a plebeian, a barbarian, a religious demagogue. Rationalism has condemned him as a raving monk—with the merit, however, of having spoken out for freedom of conscience and regenerating the Church. To many he has appeared as obscurantist—intellectually weak, mentally unbalanced—a slave of the nobility; others have praised his genius, his insight, and his biblical perception. Catholic historians, generally unsympathetic, have sometimes seen him as suffering from hallucinations, transitory dementia, or preoccupation with Satan—a monomaniac with an unfortunate temperament; as a man morally decayed, or even a seasoned criminal.

Whatever the final judgment of history may be, one cannot but admit the presence, along with his passionate temperament, of a prodigiously fertile intelligence.[1] Luther was above all an intuitive genius and, though void of systematization owing to an excess of imagination, he possessed a thrilling eloquence. His essay on Christian liberty and his devout commentary on the Magnificat bear witness to a piety that was often lyrical. It was also profound, rooted in Augustine, Paul and the Psalms. His was never the rigor of a Calvinist, and he thought less of logic than of the encounter with the saving God of Scripture. Conceiving himself as a prophet of primitive Christianity, he felt that his task was to restore to the center of Christian experience God's saving action in Christ. Christianity was for him the personal experience of being saved by Christ, and he believed that this experience was brought about less by institutions and history than by prayer and the reading of the Scriptures. There is no doubt that his language is often savage; but so is that of St. Bernard, to say nothing of St. Jerome. In many respects a conservative, Luther was by temperament a lover of civil and material order and of religious discipline.

On October 31, 1517, Luther nailed to the church door of Wittenberg his ninety-five paragraphs on indulgences, and the Protestant revolt had begun. But history does not move in sudden leaps; the way had been prepared for Luther and Lutheranism. The Church was much in need of reform and was well aware of the fact. The greed and licentiousness of many of the clergy of all ranks had become notorious. Disorder and the spirit of rebellion persisted. Clerics in concubinage and simoniacal prelates were in scandalous abundance. The four claimants to Peter's throne at the time of the Great Schism and their mutual excommunications caused a profound uneasiness and a longing for order and discipline. Some Christians even went so far as to question the value of the Papacy itself in so chaotic a situation and began to wonder if, after all, a general council might not be a more effective means of government.

In addition, at the same time that the medieval synthesis seemed to be dissolving the new humanism was awakening intellectual forces which were in some ways welcome and in other ways disquieting. A Church that had ruled with unquestioned authority throughout the Middle Ages now found itself confronted by an intellectual revolution. The general temper of the humanist renaissance, especially in Italy, often introduced paganism as an alternative to Christianity, with an inevitably deteriorating effect on the ecclesiastical and doctrinal presuppositions of the time. The rise of the *bourgeoisie* of city and town, and of the liberal intellectuals of the court and university cities, added to the general ferment.

Some historians argue also that the rise of nationalism, which profoundly altered the traditional concepts of Church-State relationship, was the chief factor in disrupting the ancient ideal of a Christian universe, wherein Pope and Emperor each enjoyed clearly defined spheres of authority. Other forces were at work to contribute to the general unrest. A new laicism was gaining strength while anti-clericalism continued to spread more and more widely. Even before Luther had proclaimed the universal priesthood of the laity a growing resentment against priest and monk had prepared the ground for a flourishing anti-authoritarianism. In the field of piety, too, mystical quietism had created a culture favorable to certain Lutheran theses. In the Low Countries especially, pietistic movements which were less institutional-minded than traditional Christianity came to flower as part of the distinctive phenomena of the age. Luther was by no means alone in his feeling that the times called for a change as other theologians voiced their dissatisfaction with a decadent scholasticism.

While the powerful middle-class watched with dismay the flood of German gold to Rome, the indifference and corruption of the clergy stirred a whole people to angry demand for a genuine reform. Pope Hadrian VI admitted with regret that the Church was suffering from detestable evils, even to the partial corruption of theology itself.

To this situation and to his own inner torments, Luther reacted with vehemence. After his sudden call to the religious life he had lived as a good monk, seeking union with God through the ascetical practices common to his day. Opposed to the "spirituals" of his community, he had sought to allay his tormenting scruples about his own salvation through fasting, prayers and docility to direction. But peace was slow in coming. The tradition of Occam, Biel, Pierre d'Ailly, the Scotist emphasis on God as personal will, all aroused in him a longing to experience the saving act of God in a direct and personal way. Disgusted with the arid scholasticism of his day, he elected to work at biblical studies and was appointed professor of theology. It was in this post, while engaged in commenting on the *Sentences* of Peter Lombard, the Psalms, and St. Paul that Luther underwent, in 1513, a spiritual experience which was to be the basis of his principle of liberation: salvation through faith, through confidence.

The Christian must renounce the vain effort to become sinless, consent to God's overwhelming mercy and allow God's saving action to forgive him while he remained a sinner. Sin will remain in man always, but the redemptive love of God will cover it over with the merits of Christ. From then on it becomes useless to preoccupy oneself with "good works," to disturb oneself concerning growth in perfection. Man will always be an unworthy servant. Let him accept the fact. Experience proves that all during his earthly sojourn he is poisoned by self-love and concupiscence, that he is genuinely a sinner. Grace, the love of God, although it brings peace, does not transform man interiorly. Luther vehemently denied the contention of Catholic theologians that grace became interior to man as a divinizing principle of life, a permanent *habit*. To him the very notion smacked of Aristotle, "that Monster," "that blind heathen," who had corrupted the biblical notion of grace as love, through the agency of the medieval doctors. The "Holy Ghost is greater than Aristotle." "Almost the whole of Aristotle's bad ethics is hostile to grace."

The passionate confidence with which Luther clung to his position that grace, the love of God, brings peace and justifies, but does not alter man's objective state, shows the force it must have had in ridding him of his personal anguish. In his doctrine that Christ's imputed justice suffices Luther is doubtless heir to nominalism. Our merits are gifts of God, and it is useless to discuss the question of coöperation with God's graces. Justification is an event, not a process. It occurs when man grasps by faith that God in Christ personally forgives him, and it need not be renewed through the sacramental channels. Baptism and the eucharist suffice—although Luther personally continued the practice of confession until the end of his life.[2]

Luther considered his true masters to be St. Paul—the Paul of Galatians and Romans—and St. Augustine. When Paul describes the conflict between concupiscence and the law, Luther recognizes his own struggles, and makes Paul's opposition to legalism his own. Elevating his personal experience of Christianity into a universally valid principle, he sees himself as the liberator of the Christian conscience. To the moral impotence of man is joined the subjective certitude of justification through faith alone. With this basic insight secure, Luther was ready to scrap indulgences—and not merely the abuses connected with them—purgatory, and the Mass. Fifteen centuries of Christian experience and theological reflection are bypassed to recover what he considered to be Pauline and evangelical truths. Christian liberty becomes his watchword. Between grace and glory the rupture is final. Heaven can never be a maturation of the gifts God imparts to the Christian, for these gifts are never really grasped by the Christian as his own. There is no inner principle of justification. Original sin has corrupted man so thoroughly that even when covered by the merits of Christ the Christian can do little but sin. God in His forgiving goodness prefers to look on the Christian's sins as venial although in fact they are grave. Only faith can save the sinner. But Luther's concept of faith is complex, since it contains the element of intellectual adherence but makes much more of the confident abandonment to Christ of the sinner in anguish, fully conscious of his inability to observe the divine law. Individualism is now supremely triumphant. As time goes on the typical Lutheran thesis becomes more sharply delineated. Free will is totally denied and man becomes simply a passive instrument in the hands of the omnipotent creator. (This thesis later Lutherans will reject.)

There is no longer any need for the sacramental system. Direct and unmediated contact with Christ the Saviour—fear, humility, and desperate abandonment to Christ—are enough. The social tones of supernatural life are muted. The sacraments of baptism and the eucharist—and Luther wished always to retain the Real

Presence—excite salutary faith in the receiver, but it is faith alone which justifies. Before the Council of Trent takes place Luther will have consolidated his fundamental theses: justification by faith alone, the radical corruption of man through original sin, the lack in man of free will, and extrinsic imputation of the merits of Christ.

Luther always felt that these radical theses were nothing but a return to evangelical teachings, long since corrupted by the Roman Church. Enamored of scriptural studies from the beginning, he felt that in returning to them he was re-exploring a field that had been abandoned. Unaware that Colet at Oxford, Lefebre at Paris, and Erasmus had preceded him in the field, he also failed to realize that he himself had read Paul through the eyes of Occam. Ironically, this prophet of Christian liberty was to hand the Church over to the state. Although he seems not to have envisaged any break with the Church at the start, his theses made this inevitable. In 1520 the Bull *Exsurge Domine* condemned forty-one propositions taken from his works. In 1521 he took his stand upon Scripture alone, denying the authority of both Pope and council, and the schism was complete.

It is obviously difficult for a Catholic to judge Luther fairly, and his own lack of system makes the task even harder. In addition, the presuppositions and misunderstandings will be many and inevitable. Since, however, the Church has formulated her Tridentine doctrine concerning sanctifying grace largely in opposition to Luther's favorite theses, the task is necessary if we are to appreciate the positions taken by the Church at the Council of Trent.

In some ways, as we have already observed, Luther was more a conservative than an iconoclast in temperament. He refused to align himself with many of the movements of his time. The need for moral reform found sympathy with him, yet he was by no means a moralist. He has, in fact, been accused of antinomianism, as has St. Paul. He gave short shrift to the humanists who were loudly proclaiming the liberation of man from the Church under another banner, condemning them all as Pelagians. The Rhineland mystics, the pietists, did not interest him. Certainly his political tendencies were not a response to the aspirations of his times. When the peasants arose in revolt he blessed their destruction with the militant cry: "Smite them, butcher as many as possible." Force was needed for healthy government—or so he believed. Even his attitude to the Church was curiously ambiguous. Wanting order, a Church in which every detail was in place, centered on obedience, he had little sympathy with extremists such as the Anabaptists. Unable to tolerate the authority of Rome, he was himself an authoritarian by nature.

Nor did Luther ever acknowledge that his theological positions were new. Instead, as we have seen, he took them as a return to the biblical world of decision and active commitment wherein man confronts God in person. His concept of faith is primarily just such an involvement of one's whole being and existence, a confident trust in the amazing—almost irrational—forgiveness of God's redeeming love in Christ.

Those who expect rational systematization and the resolution of antinomies in Luther will be disappointed. Although some have pushed his paradoxes to their logical conclusions, Luther would not necessarily have recognized them as his own. Time and again he holds to both sides of what appear logical opposites. Unlike Calvin, he is untroubled by systematic preoccupations or the need for structure. In the manner of Kierkegaard, he feels that some of the deepest insights of religion can best be expressed in paradox. His self-contradictions may disturb his students; one feels that they did not especially disturb him. His thought is biblical and can successfully maintain two antithetic moments of a problem without concern to unify them philosophically. No one can deny that theology finds it difficult to offer wholly consistent solutions to some of the grave problems this innovator boldly undertook to probe.

His contempt for scholasticism did him little service in the end; in spite of his profoundly authentic Christian insights, Luther never came to realize that these same insights, far from being denied by the teachings of the doctors of scholasticism, were in fact being completed by them. Had he better understood the positive meaning underlying scholastic formulations there might have been much more ground for reconciliation.

To take an example, Luther proclaimed that the sinner remains a sinner after justification, since he is still infected by concupiscence. This has led some to decide that Luther could not distinguish between concupiscence, temptation, and consent. When he declares that man is *simul peccator et justus,* at once a sinner and just, he seems to be reducing justification to a legal fiction. Again, Luther insists that we have full assurance of our justification before God, yet he also maintains that the justified man must continually plead with God for this gift. Steadfastly announcing that we are saved by trust alone, that we must experience the rapturous certainty of being justified by faith alone, he continually and thunderously warns that fear of the final judgment can never be eliminated from the Christian consciousness.

Even though utterly assured of justification and salvation, the Christian must somehow embrace two moments of truth: although God's gracious movement to man has justified and redeemed him, and justification is an abiding fact, His justice still rejects man as a sinner, for we are all unprofitable servants. Utter confidence is possible only because the God who first loved us while we were sinners is unchangeable and faithful. His grace may be relied on, no matter how untrustworthy we are. But this does not imply that man can be certain that God has already numbered him among the elect. Luther would have rejected such an idea at once. He denied that one can probe the mystery of election, or read the presence of grace by signs, and maintained that to take for granted that one is numbered among the elect is presumption. Nevertheless Luther called upon the Christian to believe completely in his salvation, present and to come; justified by faith, the sinner is still a sinner and always will be, but the unchanging divine initiative assures him that what God wills is his redemption. And God's fidelity cannot be invalidated by the infidelity of man.[3]

Although the sinner may never appeal to his acquired righteousness for reassurance, he must believe that he is saved now and for
the future. The reason for this is clear to Luther: God orders us
to hope. He does not invite man to trust but orders him to; hence
the certainty of salvation is evolved out of this assurance. It is the
Christian's duty to believe that God will not reject him.

For the Catholic, much of this sounds like presumption; for
Luther it would have been presumptuous for a limited creature to
distrust God's saving intentions because of his faults. To the
Catholic, the working out of salvation in fear and trembling seems
a necessity. To Luther, we have no certitude and we have every
certitude, born of trust. The position is paradoxical: we can only
trust that we have trust; if we have it we are saved; we must act
as though we had it and yet strive daily to regain it. At any rate,
it is clear that Luther never meant to assert that faith made man
certain of his election here and now, or of his effective possession
of grace, but that he must have utter trust that this is so and that
through trust it becomes so. One cannot describe this position in a
logical fashion, for it is impervious to logical categories. While grace
is both a present fact and a future certainty, the sinner who is
graced knows that he is still a sinner yet is aware also that the
author of grace is trustworthy; that his favor is not capricious.

Luther's famous thesis of justification by faith alone is equally
complex. For Luther this was the one point on which he was never
open to compromise or discussion: God freely pardons the sinner
who trusts His love in Christ. Human merit, good works are useless. Christ's redeeming work is the sole ground of our justice, and
it is not supplemented by our merits. His grace is no divinely communicated quality or habit; and although free and full forgiveness
is communicated at baptism, justification is an abiding attitude of
the Father to the trusting sinner without regard either to sins or
good works. The idea of merit must be expunged from religion, for
it leads to legalism. Man may never establish any claim upon God.
The sinner is justified solely by the divine compassion which

descends to pardon him who trusts, irrespective of his works. Does it seem irrational that God should love the unworthy? The answer is that although it transcends reason, it is the heart of the gospel message. Consequently all moralism, every shade of legalism, must be avoided, and no calculus of rewards and punishments is of any worth in the Christian perspective. Reason cannot compass the self-giving of God. The sinner truly deserves wrath, but God's justice is salvific rather than retributive, reaching out after sinners until love becomes unintelligible to reason. Does it contradict rationality, morality, the divine moral law that God should justify the ungodly, the sinner? Doubtless; but God's forgiveness acts directly through His judgment, for His judgment is "judgment and salvation," as both Old and New Testaments prove.

The Roman Church, Luther felt, had interpreted divine realities in terms of things, instead of persons, and so was unable to grasp the truth that God can justify the sinner and still have him remain a sinner. Rome's conception of grace appeared too objective; involving a kind of impersonal magic, a mechanical operation far removed from biblical categories. Grace, in Catholic theology, seemed a quasi-material thing imparted through the sacramental system.

Yet Luther by no means condemns law or good works in themselves. The concept of law is integral to St. Paul, and the concept of good works is evangelical; it is only that they do not complement the justification which comes from faith alone. Good works are the fruit of justification, valueless for eternal life but still the normal product of justification. Luther took the moral law with great seriousness and demanded obedience to it, for God hates sin and the sinner; otherwise He would be unrighteous. The law of God has the anger of God as its sanction, and He expels from His presence those who work iniquity. Consequently, when his friend Agricola wished to abolish the concept of law, Luther made a violent attack upon him. Only men who have understood the law, realized their inability to live it, and responded with Christian terror can fully grasp the doctrine of the gospel—salvation by trust.

When Agricola assumed that the rejection of legalism meant the rejection also of the law and good works, Luther replied: "It is impossible for faith to exist without assiduous, many and great works." Faith without a moral life would be a caricature, a blasphemy. But one cannot be saved by fulfilling laws and doing good works.

The antinomy is not resolved, but to those who know his forebears in theology, Luther's statements become somewhat more intelligible. Occam's voluntarism had prepared the way, by teaching that God could, if He chose, accord the beatific vision to purely human merit, and that justification is an extrinsic thing. Biel, his student, had insisted that while created grace does exist, God could justify man without imparting it, even as He could refuse to beatify those who possess grace. In this perspective the notion of merit is denatured. An act is meritorious because conformed to reason and accepted by God. If grace plays any role, it is simply that God accepts more easily an act which proceeds from His gift. The idea of grace as a sharing in the divine life is thus minimized and many Lutheran theses are anticipated in the nominalist school of theology. God, since He is omnipotent, could declare a man just while he remained a sinner. Although as a matter of fact God *does* demand grace before He declares a man just, it could as easily be otherwise. For all things rest with the *will* of God.

According to Luther, God's pardoning grace is thus not a response to any goodness in man; it is creative of that goodness, but even then, man remains a sinner totally corrupted by self-love. *Simul justus et peccator*—surely an echo of St. Augustine's: "He loved us even when He hated us" or Luther's own: "deeper than the No, and above it, the deep, mysterious, Yes."

Luther's master of novices, we are told, had quoted St. Bernard to him to relieve his scruples: "The mercy of the Lord is my merit." Luther, with his concept of the discontinuity of grace and beatitude, with his denial of an objective effect of God's redeeming love, took this to heart and denied any efficacy to merit or good works, as though such efficacy would impugn the freedom of God's love and grace. Luther could never reconcile the fact of God's love with its effective action and result in man. Nygren has noted that Protestantism fails to recognize the transforming power within human lives which Augustine and Catholicism itself maintain in a true and personal sense. The love of God for men becomes a love of God in men. The unambiguously impersonal operation of sacramental grace in the minds of those Catholics who took infant baptism as the model for all sacraments repelled Luther. But it need not have done so. In authentic Christian practice, sacramental piety has never been divorced from personal piety—it has always been its *climax,* its intensity.

Luther himself held to the sacramental principle in a mitigated way; not in the sense that the sacraments contain and confer grace but in the sense that they signify Christ's redeeming passion and resurrection as applied to the Christian. His insight was Christian— God's love in action implies in the sacrament a mutual confrontation of Christian and Christ. His failure was in not carrying the realism of divine love sufficiently far. God's redeeming action does not end with God but alters the Christian who has need of it. A true reciprocity of lover and beloved cannot be effected by the lover alone; he must alter the beloved to render him capable of union and love. Union is between two—the gift of divine love is to render the beloved, man, capable of a return of love. Auto-redemption is not entirely foreign to Catholicism; for it is the ultimate meaning of Christ's act of redemption. His saving grace is not superficial but redeems man to the depths where his liberty can collaborate with redemption. No other limit would be worthy of Christ's love or of any authentic love. Contrary to the belief of many moderns, Protestantism did not expel "things" from religion to substitute "persons." Instead it reduced the sinner, the Christian, to a "thing" incapable of giving personal response to the redemptive love of God in Christ through God's gracious communication of His life. In despoiling man of his power to say "yes" to the divine invitation it underestimates the efficacy of Christ's redemption to associate with its power the action of the man who has been enabled by God to coöperate with his own salvation exclusively through the loving grace of God. Melancthon put it pithily when he said that grace is good will and not medicine. It would, however, be a curious kind of good will that would refuse medicine when needed.[4]

As we have noted, it is only at first glance that the Lutheran position of salvation by faith alone seems to ignore the importance of good works, and that the classic Lutheran opposition between gospel and law implies that the law is valueless. The gospel announces the good news of salvation and requires the risk, the leap of trust, even while the despair and pain of sin remain. The law, it seems, is powerless. Yet Luther does not make light of sin, and the law has a function, although in his thought it can never be fulfilled by empirical man, who is incapable of that disinterested love which the law requires. In all things sinful man puts self-seeking first, and this is the root of all his sinning. Hence the Christian has reason to stand trembling before the justice of God. Luther lays heavy stress on the biblical doctrine of the wrath of God, the holy and immutable judgment of God upon sin. Between the holy will of God and man's sinful will there is an abyss, and grace does not close it. God's wrath and His righteousness stand unchangeably opposed to sin; but to Luther the justice of God is not vindicative, its function is not to reward the good and punish the evil, as a moralist might suppose. It is not so much punitive as salvific, and here Luther produces a formula derived in part from an Old Testament theme. God's justice is not an impartial verdict against the sinner but a creative force for forgiveness.

The law's function is to bring man to despair, so that he may grasp the redeeming mercy of God. This is part of God's loving intention, so that His seeking of man may not be in vain. The law is a pedagogue, revealing our impotence to observe it and our secret collaboration with our own inability to keep it. When it has shown us our self-idolatry and brought us to despair in ourselves, we become aware at the same time of the wrath of God directed against our sinfulness and of His willingness to rescue us from despair. The moral law demands absolute fulfillment, but man cannot give it. Luther takes the moral law with extreme seriousness, and in his view the gospel freedom is not pretext for avoiding law. But in the end all is grace, since man cannot fulfill the law.

What Luther fears most is a concept of merit based exclusively on human pretensions. Since he excludes from man any participation in the divine life, any infused gift of grace, nothing is left but human merit, and this is clearly discontinuous with eternal life. So strong a reaction against Pelagianism would be justified if we granted Luther's extrinsic conception of grace. The desire to earn one's own salvation by unaided human effort is one of the oldest heresies. Luther does not succeed in resolving this antinomy either. One must observe the law, and indeed the biblical concepts of reward and punishment are too explicit to be ignored. Paul insists on obedience to law, and Matthew's Gospel represents our judgment in terms of reward. Having removed from redeemed man the inner principle of merit, a share in the divine nature, Luther holds onto both horns of the dilemma. Good works and the law are obligatory; they are also impossible and useless. Faith alone justifies. The "new man" will discover the law within and the Holy Spirit will perform its works through him. To Luther justification by faith alone does not lead to quietism but to authentic morality. "We will take our ease and do no good work, but be content with faith." "Not so, ye wicked men. God gives no one his grace that he may lie down and do nothing worth any more." Man must labor to produce good works, but he is aware that they are valueless.

It was against this background of paradoxical theses that the Council of Trent was to define the Christian position on grace and merit, free will, and man's capacity to observe the law and the teachings of the gospel.[5]

In his early attempts to gain salvation Luther had viewed the work of salvation in semi-Pelagian fashion as something to be undertaken by man and merely crowned or completed by God. In 1513 his despair arising from this position was changed to exultant joy, for he came to see that salvation was exclusively the work of God. Man had vainly sought to merit grace, but the fact that he could not do so was no need for despair. Grace, far from having to be merited, was itself the only possible source of merit. The gospel gives the answer to man's powerlessness to achieve salvation—what man cannot accomplish God, in Christ, has done for him. If then we are not saved by ourselves but by Another, our immediate duty is to trust in Him. Salvation is a grace, a gift of God, not the work of man. Therefore man can be saved by faith in God the Saviour, and by this means alone. Faith alone must save us; otherwise we would have to add something, and that addition would result in the denial of the essential thing. For, if believing in the principle of the saving action of God we were obliged to add something of our own initiative, the result would be that we would have to accomplish our salvation in part, in the hope that God would do the rest. Either we are not saved by divine grace, acknowledged and accepted by faith, or this grace is the sole cause of our salvation and faith is the sole means of approach to it.

This is the cause of Luther's rejection of the notion of salvation by faith and works. But we must take a closer look at his position. In principle the idea being rejected is that we have to add our personal contribution of activity independently of grace and faith. But if human works are necessary, we are then saved by neither faith nor grace. Faith in divine grace would only assure us that a part of our salvation need no longer concern us. The conclusion Luther reached is that all in our salvation comes to us by faith.

To Luther's contention that all comes to us in grace from God Calvin added the idea that all tends to His glory. If it is God who does all, it is He alone who is sovereign. The difficulties that had faced Luther in his attempt to "merit" salvation were caused by his losing sight of the transcendence of God, whose irruption into history is what constitutes the whole of Christianity. Man sought means of his own to merit the salvation that only God could confer because the idea of a transcendent God separated from all creatures by an infinite gulf had been lost. Man had come to the point of putting the creature on the level of the Creator, which is why he expected from himself what could be sought and found only in the Lord. Calvin stressed that we must see God not as one source of life among others—ourselves, institutions, human or created agencies; God is not only the first among beings, but the sovereign, and in a sense the only, Being. All reality, seen from the specifically religious standpoint, can come only from Him, just as all reality can have no end other than Him. Thus all glory must be given solely to God. The only kind of knowledge of God that counts is that which makes us recognize the sovereign power of God and so to devote ourselves, entirely and exclusively, to His glory.

Originally, good works were not meaningless to Calvin any more than they were to Luther. The good works of the Christian were not a partial or in any way independent cause of justification and salvation, something added to the pure gift of God, but were the normal products of this gift. Christ, who justifies us, offers us both justification and sanctification. The attainment of one must be accomplished by the attainment of the other. "Thus in being justified man is sanctified," Calvin wrote. "Thus we are not justified without works, but yet not by works, since our participation in Christ by which we are justified includes sanctification as well as justice."

The aim of both Luther and Calvin in personal religious conduct was to turn the individual entirely from trust in humanity that he might rest absolutely in God. To conceive of salvation as a grace received through the divine word by faith implies that there is not only a personal decision on the part of the individual but, occasioning this, a previous divine attention *to* the individual. There is a divine interest which considers the individual and in a certain way makes him different from everyone else. Thus the true Protestant individualism is one that implies a real and fundamental awareness of something over and above him, and is a positive attitude based on a vivid appreciation of this relationship. The relationship of man and God must be face-to-face and one-to-one. Man is not saved as a member of a group, the Church, the Mystical Body, but as an individual. Thus his relations with God should be basically on the individual level. The works and intentions of others are no aid to him if he personally does not respond to the unique love of God. Faith is the discovery of this divine love. The realization that this love comes not from any merit, and even in spite of actual demerit, solves the problem of man's unworthiness. But the love of God comes to him who loves God. Christ has said that He shall make Himself known to him who loves Him. But the knowledge of Christ is also the love of Christ.

Any trace of authoritarianism naturally awoke the anger of Luther, for to him a religious act performed because of compelling authority was worse than blasphemy. The only thing that counts in the sight of God is a free, personal act, accomplished in the most interior as well as exterior freedom. Consequently, anything which violates this liberty of conscience undermines the very possibility of the only religion acceptable to God, that of a man who gives himself freely.[6]

Since salvation has been attained through grace given to us by God and since this has been revealed to us in the Bible, it is understandable that the Bible plays so important a part in the life of the Protestant. The Bible is not merely the historical relation of the life of Christ but a living contact of the individual with the "Word." The Bible shows the great Christian truths as saving realities, as intimate experiences, and as governing the whole of life. It is by coming into individual, personal touch with these realities that man establishes contact with the "Word."

The main positive elements of the Reformation are of themselves admissible. Man is not saved by his own works; all glory is owed to God; the Bible is God speaking to each of us. The difficulty is that these positive elements are joined with negative ones and were distorted in controversy.

It is unfortunate that the positive Christian insights of Luther became deformed through the stiffening of positions engendered by controversy. His concept of the justified sinner did not originally imply a great deal more than the truth that every victory of sin over man's natural powers must be repaired by the saving power of God acting through human weakness. The positive truth he affirmed with such boldness had been stated many times in the past by the Roman Church: God is the author of our salvation and we can trust His love. The Second Council of Orange had been categorical on this point. Our powerlessness to meet God's demands by our own strength, together with the acknowledgment that the power to accomplish His will is given us by Another, is a basic Christian truth.[7]

Originally Luther conceived of faith as closely bound up with love; it is only later that he rejects vehemently the scholastic distinction between dead faith and faith formed by charity. Grace was not seen by him at first as a legal fiction dispensing from action but as an irresistible power set in motion by Christ to transform those who donate themselves to Him without reserve. It is Christ who will create within man the new creature, to be there renewed from day to day through the grace of Christ. Luther's basic intuition of man's utter dependence upon the Lord, in its positive affirmations, is a central Catholic truth. The negative formulas that logic and argument developed—the rejection of good works, the concept of extrinsic justification—are neither necessary conclusions to his positions nor expressions of his central intuitions.

In the course of history Luther came to be characterized at least as much by these negations as by his living insights, but this does not seem necessary. At first a religion of faith was contrasted with an external religion, a pure conformism, a legitimate emphasis being placed upon a religion that engaged the deepest strata of man's soul in an individual, highly personal commitment. This emphasis on the individual was not illegitimate in Christian thought, which had never conceived of man's response to God purely in terms of uniform religious customs, accepted rites, with no attention to individual decision. Luther's attempt to free the individual and to re-establish contact with Christ was valid insofar as it was an attempt to free him from mechanized and legalized systems of practices. But in rejecting the complexities of ecclesiastical organization, in seeking freedom from an external Church, his thought risked and found deviation. Had he simply underscored his realization that religion always implies a personal recognition, that man is personally involved by God's free action in approaching him, and that he must detach himself from self to recognize total dependence on God's sovereign Lordship, his teachings would have been sound. Religion that involves no personal commitment is indeed superficial, if not unreal.

There is a fairly clear pattern discernible in the way that Luther's positive insights were gradually deformed by the negative elements joined to them in the course of his quarrels with Catholic theologians. His concept of faith is originally a response of a man to the love of Christ in such wise that love could not possibly be excluded from it. Christ loves us not only in spite of our lack of merit but even despite our sinfulness. Faith that becomes aware of this love grasps its own unworthiness and abandons itself without reserve to the love that cures its sinfulness. Far from proclaiming man's autonomy such a faith recognizes its own utter dependence and implies charity or love. It is beyond question that, as he first understood it, Luther's justifying faith implied the love of gratitude and led to a total self-commitment to Christ and His precepts. Certainly Luther's later rejections of the formula "faith formed by love" are notorious; but it may be that in rejecting this formula Luther is simply discarding the idea that justifying faith, to be such, requires a *natural* love of God, derived not from the grace of Christ but from the powers of unaided nature. Faith is a love that is pure response to the gratuitous love of God in Christ which anticipates our faith and love and, in fact, empowers us to have them. However, later emphasis on the negative aspects (the *alone* of *faith alone*) deformed Luther's original intentions.

His attacks on good works, begun in order to purify religion of ritualism and to emphasize a religion of the spirit, suffered the same fate. Christ too had stressed, and the prophets before Him, that man must give his heart to God, translating this gift of self into loving action towards man and God. The Catholic Church had always maintained that a religion of legalism which implied no authentic and interior self-donation, be it ever so scrupulous in observation of law and credal orthodoxy, was a vain and empty thing.

The master-principle of Christian spirituality had always been interior charity, with the firm belief that no sacramental or ritual element could absolve the individual from the personal effort to make faith vital and individual, touching the heart and will of man.

Insofar as Luther and the other Reformers sought to renew adherence to these primitive Christian insights the Church did not and could not oppose them. But the further the conflict with Rome advanced, the more the negative principles of Lutheranism emerged. That no change is effected by grace, that saving faith is not joined to love, that interior religion requires freedom from the Church, that good works are useless even when done in grace— all these unscriptural positions were firmly rejected by the Church at Trent. The sovereignty of God is affirmed again, but not such a sovereignty as obliterates man.[8]

Imprisoned in a philosophic framework of decadent Occamism, Luther could neither unify his insights with the rest of Christian tradition nor remain true to them. A grace which really transforms man is almost unthinkable in Occam's philosophy, affected as it was by empiricism and nominalism. God could only intervene to change us by changing Himself. To remain a gift from God, grace logically must remain utterly extrinsic, since real relations between God and the creature are unintelligible. The confusion of God's transcendent sovereignty with arbitrary freedom, the sovereignty of will over being, truth and goodness, are legitimate consequences of the nominalist idea that God can justify man while leaving him without grace, "accepting" him as just. Man is then beyond good and truth. To such a pass the vitiated scholasticism to which Luther was heir brought him at last.

It is ironic to realize that in the course of history Luther's intentions would be so perverted. What began as a hymn to the unassailable power of grace finished as a Pelagian confidence in human powers. Misplaced emphasis on the authority of the word of Scripture ended in a Bible so humanized as to be almost without divine inspiration. And in some cases, with the espousal of a rigid authoritarianism, Christian liberty ceased to exist.

It was indeed a lamentable situation that Luther's ambitious reform program had provoked. At his death on February 18th, 1546, Luther's Church had established itself in many parts of Christendom and had divided Europe in a catastrophic way. Sweden, Denmark, Norway were lost to the Church together with the Duchy of Prussia in Poland and many princely states of Germany.

NOTES

1. H. Grisar, *Luther* (St. Louis, Herder, 1913), pp. 157-172.
2. P. Vignaux, "Nominalisme," *D.T.C.*, cols. 770-779.
3. Rondet, *Gratia Christi*, p. 258.
4. L. Cristiani, "Réforme," *D.T.C.*, col. 2062.
5. J. Paquier, "Luther," *D.T.C.*, col. 1231.
6. H. Baudrillart, "Calvin," *D.T.C.*, cols. 1398-1402.
7. L. Bouyer, *The Spirit and Forms of Protestantism* (Westminster, Newman, 1956), ch. 1.
8. *Ibid.*, pp. 166-176.

APPENDIX II

THE COUNCIL OF TRENT

THIRTY YEARS AFTER Luther's public attack on indulgences and seventeen years after the confession of Augsburg the fathers of the Council of Trent met to formulate Catholic doctrine in the face of the Reformers. Previous efforts at reconciliation had failed. After his publication of the ninety-five paragraphs on indulgences Luther had engaged in a written controversy with the Roman theologians, had appealed to "a better-informed Pope" and then to the Pope in a general council. Finally, in July of 1520 he rejected the authority of Rome. Although Pope Leo X had condemned certain theses concerning indulgences, Purgatory and other points of doctrine in 1520, it was not until Luther had refused to accept the authority of the Pope, tradition and the Catholic teaching on the sacraments that the full force of his teachings became evident.

The Council of Trent now undertook to examine Luther's central thesis, justification by faith alone, and having done so, to state the Catholic teaching on the matter in a decree that is a model of balance and authority. The final draft of the decree, however, was not arrived at without lengthy and even acrimonious debate.

Wisely enough it was decided to inaugurate the work of the council with the efforts of congregations of theologians. These scholars, while not of episcopal rank, numbered among them some of the most distinguished experts of the time on patristic and biblical theology, outstanding figures such as the Dominican Dominic Soto and the Franciscan Alfonso de Castro. Their function was to debate important topics among themselves and to provide information to those of episcopal rank.[1]

The second stage of proceedings gathered together all those who were actually entitled to vote, and in this stage each member cast his official *votum* on the matter at hand, the dogmatic issue or the disciplinary question. At first the meetings took place in the Palazzo Prato, but as the number of bishops increased it was considered wise to transfer to the Church of Saint Mary Major.

Professional theologians at times worked directly with the legates in preparing decrees, but more often this work was entrusted to commissions chosen by the council to formulate the decrees. As regards determination of the programme and proposing material for discussion, each member of the council, including the representatives of accredited powers, could make suggestions. As secretary, the council was fortunate in having Massarelli, to whose diligence we owe the carefully drawn up protocols and much information about the council.

One of the major threats to to the council was, of course, the unstable military situation. The Italians had not come too willingly to Trent in the first place. When news came that the Protestant General Scharltin had been triumphant in the first engagements of the war of Schmalkalden, and had actually succeeded in seizing the pass at Ebrenberg, consternation broke out at the council, and the Italians wanted to move it to a safer spot. But Madruzzo and the legates held off that contingency. Charles the Fifth, with the assistance of papal troops, made the move unnecessary, and the council was able to proceed to discuss the great topic of justification.

A further reason for the length of time it took to arrive at the final decree was the stand taken by Seripando, the General of the Augustinians, who was most unwilling to have the council by-pass certain of his theories if this could be avoided. His opinion was the rather pessimistic one that Adam's fault had left men in profound ignorance—"sons of wrath," indocile to the Holy Spirit.

This viewpoint, along with his theory of a "double justice," was to occasion considerable lively debate. According to the theory (which we have treated at various points in this book), man must rely on a double justice; he is indeed justified interiorly by the communicated justice—the grace—of Christ, but so terrible are the ravages of sin within even the just that all but the great saints require another justice. At the divine tribunal men must rely far more on the justice and merits of Christ, which God imputes to them, than on their own prayers or justice. Man, it seems, is not fully justified by sacramental absolution or by baptism.

In point of fact it was this very idea of extrinsic justification that lay at the heart of all the Reformers' negations, and this the council decisively rejected, maintaining that man is justified by a justice which is proper and interior to each one, poured into his soul by the Holy Spirit. The final decree, promulgated on January 13, 1547, showed the effects of the prolonged discussions. Opposed alike to the radical pessimism of the Reformers and to the Pelagian tendencies of the Humanists, it was the result of many previous drafts. On June 17th of the preceding year the decree on original sin had been accepted by the Fathers of the council, and on June 29th a preliminary draft of the decree on justification had been submitted for their approval. A month later the first draft of the final decree, elaborated by a commission of four members and containing twenty-one chapters, was submitted. Theologians continued their debates, and the Fathers discussed the positions at length, until Seripando on the 11th of August submitted a decree which was later so retouched by Roman theologians that he declared he could scarcely recognize his work. Nevertheless this decree was submitted to the Fathers of the council, and in its general lines was retained in the final decree.

Certain Catholic theologians, moved by fear of Lutheran determinism, came to accept a version of human liberty quite unpalatable to those of the Augustinian tradition. However, a moderate Augustinian position was finally adopted, the council insisting upon the gift character of final perseverance and rejecting the Calvinistic position that grace, once possessed, could not be lost. The sinner, it declared, may lose grace not only by a sin against faith but also by any grave sin. Although in sin, he remains a member of the Church and may retain authentic faith, which may serve to bring him back to grace through the sacraments.[2]

While the council did not accept any variety of the theory of double justice, certain questions disputed among Catholics were left unsettled: whether grace is really identified with charity or really distinct from it; whether there exist infused moral virtues; whether the works which precede justification are meritorious of justification in equity; whether certain virtues are infused before justification. Preferring not to favor any particular school of theology, the council proceeded to establish what was certain and must be held by all Catholics. Consequently it emphasized sharply the two fundamental Catholic theses: (1) justification is not something extrinsic to man but is an inner transformation, an ontological change, which implies a created gift of grace really communicated to him; (2) man genuinely coöperates through his free will in the work of his own justification and, with the grace of Christ, must merit his final reward. Fallen in Adam, man must be reborn in Christ through baptism. Although insisting, in opposition to the Lutheran claim, that his justification is not accomplished without his free coöperation, the council reiterated the primitive Christian doctrine that man can do nothing in the order of salvation without the grace of Christ. With Luther and earlier councils, it maintained that the natural efforts of man, unaided by grace, do not advance his progress to grace and salvation; but it insisted that man's will is not therefore passive or inert. Once called by the first grace of God, which is in no sense merited, man must freely coöperate with it. The primacy is always with grace; the initiative is always God's. But granting that God has called man through no merit of his, man must then dispose himself for justification by free coöperation, aware of his wretchedness and sinfulness and responding with the detestation of his sins, with fear and hope and some beginning of love for God.

Faith is indeed necessary. Although it cannot justify man without hope and charity, the normal accompaniments of a lively faith, the importance of its role in justification is clearly depicted. Faith is not merely a blind commitment, a trust in the power of God to justify the sinner whose condition remains unchanged, but a vital commitment to the message of Christian revelation.

When it came to the question of the subjective certitude of justification, the council rejected the Lutheran "assurance," pointing out that, short of a private revelation, no one can be so certain of his own justification as to exclude all fear of error.

Justification is not only a genuine remission of sins but a profound interior transformation of man by which he is enriched with the presence of the indwelling God, becomes intrinsically just, a friend and son of God, and the heir to eternal life. He is justified by an interior gift which the Holy Spirit diffuses in his heart, and this gift remains in him as a permanent principle, bringing with it the three supernatural virtues of faith, hope and charity.[3]

In the second edition which preceded the final edition of the text, Seripando had labored valiantly to defend his theory of a double justice. Thirty-two theologians had held to the opinion that man is justified by an inner principle without any further extrinsic imputation of the merits of Christ. Five theologians, of whom three belonged to the order of the Hermits of St. Augustine, had declared an inner principle insufficient and the imputation of Christ's merits indispensable. Seripando observed with a certain sharpness that almost the entire vote was against his thesis. In the third edition of the text he made another unsuccessful attempt to obtain its insertion. On the 26th and 27th of November he again intervened but again failed. The theory had been placed by Seripando under the protection of Cajetan, Pighi, Pflug and Contarini. It was perhaps the opposition of the Jesuit Laynez, who marshalled twelve arguments against it, that was the decisive influence in its defeat.

Seripando, stressing the inescapable reality of the mediocre Christian whose life is filled with imperfections, maintained that there exists a truly inherent justice which renders us formally just, but that the mediocre would do better on the judgment day to trust in the imputed justice of Christ. Although the council did not accept this position, neither did it condemn it explicitly. What it did was to condemn the theory of imputed justice, but only in the Lutheran sense. That is to say, the council simply opposed the ancient Catholic tradition to the Lutheran idea of forensic justice and rejected the latter. We are by no means justified independently of the justice of Christ; but His justice is not the *formal* inherent cause of our justification. The grace which we receive is not a pure imputation, not even merely the remission of sins. It is not just a favor of God but an internal reality which the Holy Spirit pours into our soul.

At first Seripando defended the position that the justice of Christ does become ours, not because it informs or assists us, but because it is communicated to us by the sacraments, which make up for what is lacking in us by acting somewhat in the same fashion as suffrages for the dead. Suffrages offered for the dead become their property and supply for their insufficiencies. Later he modified this position. Vigorously rejecting any understanding of the imputed justice of Christ that would be *entirely* extrinsic, with no inherent justice, Seripando argued that man's justice derives from Christ's but inheres formally in his soul. Here the influence of nominalism is clearly at work. It is not habitual or sanctifying grace which first makes us pleasing to God; God must first, by an act of His will, have accepted us as pleasing to Him, just as the Father in the gospel accepted the Prodigal Son. Only later is the son clothed with the festive garment. There is then a double effect of Christ's justice: the grace which permits us to act meritoriously and the acceptation by God of our works; both of these effects are gratuitous. Hence too there is a double justice, that of grace and the works that flow from grace and that of Christ which induces

God to accept these good works. In refusing to subscribe to such a nominalist position, the council greatly clarified the notion of merit.[4]

Declaring that the justified Christian has the power to grow in grace, the council stated that justification admits of degrees, depending entirely on the good pleasure of God and the coöperation of man. In spite of his weakness, the justified man is the friend of God, who will not desert him unless man rejects Him. He must and he can observe the law and the commandments, although without an extraordinary privilege he cannot remain free from all venial sins. He must coöperate with his own salvation, and it is by no means sinful for him to hope for a recompense for his good works. If he falls into serious sin, he can be restored to grace through the sacrament of penance, which requires contrition, confession and satisfaction.

In the 16th chapter of the sixth session, on merit, we have one of the most important statements of the council. The very idea of merit, utterly repugnant to the Reformers, had been bitterly attacked by them. In reply the council set out to show that our merits are at once the gift of God and the results of man's free coöperation. In the eyes of all theologians the good works of man done after justification are meritorious *de condigno,* in strict justice, and since this merit is owing to the merits of Christ, it does not diminish His glory but augments it. Many of the Fathers, convinced with St. Augustine that our merits can be reduced to a gift of God, were content with the thought of the divine mercy. It was here that Seripando aided the council greatly. His formulae, derived from the principles of St. Augustine and St. Bernard, accented the fact that our merits are at once truly ours and truly gifts of God.

The entire gamut of Catholic opinion was covered in discussion before the council adopted its final formula. Some of the Fathers resisted the idea that man can demand a reward of God in justice. But the Dominican Gaspard Rey went to the heart of the matter in remarking that by grace the Christian is incorporated into Christ as the branch in the vine; our works flow from a divine stem. In themselves our works are mediocre, but if one considers the grace that produces them, then they are seen to have value before God. This distinction was presented in discussions over and over again, by the Carmelite Taborel and the Jesuit Laynez, and the final decree of the council evidently took it into consideration. Christ is actively present in the soul of the regenerated Christian as the head in the members, the vine in the branches. His influence is poured into our actions and is indispensable if they are to be meritorious. The Christian may enjoy a legitimate confidence along with humility and recognition of his own imperfections. Because the justice of Christ is not simply imputed to us in an extrinsic fashion but actually communicated to us so that we have a real participation in His life, our works give us a true right to a heavenly reward.[5]

The declaration of the council on merit is a supreme acknowledgment of the *reality* of the supernatural life. The basis of merit is a gratuitous promise of God mercifully accorded to us so that in a sense "all is grace"; to obtain that eternal reward one must trust in God's mercy, making use of human freedom to assent to it. We are living members of Christ able to produce works conformed to the will of God and truly worthy of reward. But this in no way detracts from the glory of Christ. For we can say with truth that grace is "ours" and yet it is Christ's. Ours insofar as it is a gift inherent in our soul, it yet remains a *divine* gift and God is the living source who communicates it to us. What is true of grace is true of merit, its fruit. *Cum Deus coronat merita nostra, nihil aliud coronet nisi munera sua:* "in crowning our merits, God crowns His gifts" (Augustine, *Epist.* 194). *Eorum velit esse merita quae sunt ipsius dona:* "the goodness of God is so great that He wished His gifts to become man's merits" (Augustine, *Epist.* 194).

The moderate tone of the entire section on justification is noteworthy. While stress is put on the human activity of man, the gift character of grace was firmly retained, and thus traditional positions were reaffirmed. Obviously, where the Reformers had remained close to Scripture there was less danger of their erring, and in some cases the council stressed the truth in the Lutheran positions which had often misapprehended Roman doctrine.

Thus the Lutheran insistence that man is at once a sinner and justified, if correctly understood, can be reconciled with the Tridentine position. The power of sin, the temptation to sin, concupiscence, remain in man even after justification, but in a different way. Sin engages man in a struggle, but the victory is assured through the grace of Christ, internally possessed. The justified man is a new creature, no longer what he was in his previous condition. He is not at once a sinner and a saint with the co-equal powers of grace and sin inhabiting him, nor a new man in whom the forces of evil are simply balanced off by grace, nor one established in a kind of unstable equilibrium between grace and sin, but a being in whom the influence of the law of sin, while remaining, has been neutralized by Christ's grace. The council does not deny the persistence in justified man of an inclination to sin, but stresses that the justified man is a new being with the radical power to overcome sin. God's merciful judgment has produced an effect in man and is manifested in the created gift of grace which renews man internally. Where the Reformers remained closest to the sources of revelation, as for example, in their affirmations of the saving and gratuitous initiative of God in Christ, Tridentine theology did not quarrel with them. God's merciful judgment, His uncreated initiative in saving man, are part of Christian tradition, and Trent never attempted to deny it. But it emphasized against the Reformers the fact that man's vital, internal activity is required as he passes from the state of sin to that of justice.

Neither did Trent minimize the Lutheran insistence upon confidence in God and faith in His salvific message. Man can grasp God's saving activity only by faith, which is the root of all justification. Only by faith in God's word can we come to realize the absolutely gratuitous initiative of God in Christ which puts man in a wholly new situation with regard to God. Because man responds to the gift of faith and accepts his divine vocation, the freedom of God's action is in no wise diminished. The reply of man is supported and effected by grace itself. Hence the importance of faith cannot be too highly stressed, since it is a fundamental attitude of response to God's revelation. It is only by holding as true God's revelation, and acting as befits this message of salvation, that man gives an adequate response to the Person revealing. Although Trent rejects any absolute subjective certitude of one's own salvation, it does not minimize the role of faith as belief in the message or of confidence in the Person who speaks.[6]

Not without reason has it been said that the religious cleavage which split the body of the Church so disastrously could have been prevented, or made to take a different turn, if only this decree on justification had been promulgated years before by the Fifth Lateran Council. Trent was actually, as history was to demonstrate, a great landmark in the history of the Church. It had been begun as a joint effort on the part of the Emperor and the Pope to settle the disturbing situation, and in its early period had looked especially to Germany, where the disunity was greatest. But it far surpassed, in its dogmatic importance, temporary questions. The dogmatic discussions give a fairly complete treatment of questions which no council had dealt with fully before. It is perhaps unfortunate that Calvin did not receive so full a treatment as might have been hoped for, but Luther and Zwingli were dealt with carefully and the Catholic positions outlined in some detail.[7]

The council proved a difficult and an expensive enterprise. From the beginning it consumed almost a tenth of the papal income, and in the last period expenses mounted so that nearly three times the original sum was involved.

Trent was an answer to the pressure that arose on all sides for a renewal of the Church from within, and an official statement of Catholic tradition to the problems raised by the Reformers. By no means simply a restatement without examination of medieval practices, it was a genuine counter-reformation, which embodied many principles of reform concerning the pastoral care of souls and of ecclesiastical discipline. What it accomplished was considerable. It established no divisions where divisions did not already exist, and it did not seek to favor one school of theologians in the Church at the expense of another.

On January 28, 1564, the Pope confirmed the decrees of Trent and gave them the force of law. Moreover, Pius IV created a special congregation to see to it that Trent's decrees were properly interpreted and enforced. Pius V sent throughout the world copies of the decrees of the council, and its influence reached even America and Africa.

The Papacy wisely invoked its authority to see to it that these decrees were fulfilled and executed in all parts of the world, and Trent's contribution to Catholic teaching entered the mainstream of Christian thinking. This council, which endured so long and treated of such delicate and vital questions, was to remain a monumental achievement, a model of prudence and thoroughness.

NOTES

1. Rondet, *Gratia Christi*, p. 279.
2. Jedin, *Papal Legate at the Council of Trent, Cardinal Seripando*, pp. 359 ff.
3. *Ibid.*, ch. xx. Cf. J. Rivière, "Justification," *D.T.C.*, 2167-2168.
4. J. Hefele and H. Leclercq, *Histoire des Conciles* (Paris, Letouzey et Ané, 1938), T. IX, pp. 311-314.
5. Hefele-Leclercq, *op. cit.*, T. X, pp. 91-103.
6. *Ibid.*, pp. 157-162.
7. Rondet, *op. cit.*, pp. 277-278.

APPENDIX III

GRACE IN THE EASTERN CHURCH

THE PERSPECTIVE of the oriental Church on sanctifying grace is somewhat different from that of the western Church. This is a distinction not of opposition but of emphasis only, based on a different philosophical orientation. The philosophy of the Fathers of the eastern Church has been consistently Platonic, and even today Russian theologians are more Platonic than Aristotelian in conceiving religious and ascetical truths. Western theologians, however, have always had a strong affinity for the categories of Aristotle and St. Thomas, and have, in fact, canonized them. Nevertheless, one should add that St. Thomas and the great scholastics of the western tradition frequently have included in their syntheses the greater part of the oriental intuitions. This is especially true of those scholastics before nominalism who were influenced strongly by the Fathers, and thoroughly imbued with their doctrines. The western philosophy of man and the western categories of causality, action and effect often sound somewhat strange to the oriental way of thinking. Consequently, one should expect a difference of accent in the explanation of grace as it is given in the East and as it is heard in the West. Yves Congar has analyzed in a few brief pages the differences between the oriental and the western Church concerning man's deification. Stressing the fact that the Orient uses different philosophical categories in its study of man and of God, he argues that the result is a different tone of spirituality and a different approach to mysticism and to many theological problems.[1]

Eastern theology sees within God an absolutely incomprehensible and supreme essence, which could be considered a supra-essence and which is utterly unknowable by any form of human knowledge. Western theologians are familiar with this view from the writings of Dionysius the Areopagite, who stresses the *via negativa* in his approach to knowledge of God. For him God is beyond all categories and remains incomprehensible to the human mind. The oriental Church, however, distinguishes over and against this supra-essence of God, certain divine, uncreated energies within the Godhead which can be known by man. When experiencing mystical graces or divine inspirations man is put in contact with these uncreated essential energies of God but not with His supra-essence, which remains hidden in an impenetrable darkness. Even the spirit which has been divinized by grace, since it is a created spirit, cannot penetrate this unknowable realm. Hence, we attain our knowledge of God in a highly negative fashion, and the mystery of the three divine Persons remains closed to us.

Latin theology, on the contrary, emphasizes the fact that the beatific vision is the term of the supernatural life and has even conceived the possibility that certain chosen ones, such as the Blessed Virgin or Moses, have been favored by a mystical experience amounting to a transitory vision of the divine essence. Obviously the distinction between the eastern and western schools of thought in this matter is not that the theologians of the West would seek to diminish the concept of God's transcendence; it is that they do not make a fundamental distinction, as the eastern theologians do, between the supra-essence and the essential energies of God.

Moreover, the oriental philosophy—which, as we have said, is drawn primarily from Plato—admits in man a *nous,* or divine spark of intelligence, essentially ordained to the contemplation of the world of ideas, the divine world superior to the sensible world. Whereas the Aristotelian philosopher and the western theologian admit this element of the divine in man and on occasion even define man as a capacity for God, still western philosophy orientates man primarily towards knowledge gained through his senses. To the eastern theologian progressive purification in the spiritual life generally means a devotion to contemplation of the divine world of ideas, so that divinization is an entry into that sphere of life as properly divine, with a share in the conditions of that life, especially immortality.

Since the philosophical presuppositions of Platonism find themselves incorporated in the mystical theology of the Orient, there is present in it the doctrine that Christ has come to restore all things in Himself and to communicate to us a share in His intelligence. But it is also understood that even *before* the redemption God had created man in His image. Having produced his body from the slime of the earth He breathed upon man and gave him a share in His divine and immortal life. Hence, man not only shares in the divine intelligence but is ordered to the divine because he retains this likeness to God. He is ordered to a life properly divine, one of immortality and incorruptibility. By *nature* already an image of God in the summit of his being—his spirit—his destiny is to realize fully his likeness to God through grace and enjoy the conditions of divine life. This is his divinization, for this is his entry into the light that surrounds God in his essence. Man is an image of God and shares somehow in the divine being by *nature*.

Obviously no western theologian would speak in precisely these terms, since, as we have noted, western theology does not make a distinction between the inaccessibility of God and His energies or powers. When the oriental Church speaks of a natural sharing in the divinity it does not mean to deny the transcendence of God but rather to grant to man a natural share in the uncreated divine energies. Hence the oriental Church can speak of a certain natural consubstantiality of man with God and can refer to man in his natural state as God-bearing, as an image of God. Adam, the perfect type of humanity, had such a share in the divine nature.

Resuming all of created nature in himself, Adam submitted it and the life of the senses to a higher life of the intelligence in himself. The fall of Adam was not only a sin on his part, it had repercussions which troubled the cosmic unity. The meaning of the world of the senses—the concrete, existent world—consisted in its being spiritualized through the intelligence of man. Since the order of creation has been radically compromised by Adam's fault it is unable, in its present state, to be brought to its full destiny of divine immortality and incorruptibility.

The Greek Fathers were persistently conscious of a nostalgia for the state of affairs in which the cosmos, the body, the world of the senses are submitted to the divine element in man and ordered to his incorruptible divine destiny. In their conception of things the task of redeeming man is not only to bring creation back to the faithful mirroring of God's perfections, but also to fulfill it, to complete it, to recommence the divinizing process interrupted by Adam. The Holy Spirit is to restore the similitude shattered by the sin of Adam and to plunge man once again into the divine world. Hence, the work of Christ is viewed primarily as a *recapitulatio,* a restoration of the entire universe as well as humanity to God, so that the incarnation of the Eternal Word, which begins the process, has as its purpose to communicate the deifying strength of the Holy Spirit to all creation, to sanctify and elevate it.

Another element in the oriental position is the concept of the incarnation as a taking up of the process of divinization concerning which man still feels nostalgia. The western Church frequently views the redemption of Christ as a reparation, a buying back of man from sin, an offering made to God to induce Him to grant pardon to man and to restore the lost gift of grace, the relationship of friendship with God. But the oriental Church sees in the redemptive incarnation rather a re-spiritualization of all nature and a re-creation of man from within. All things are recapitulated in Christ and thus find their true destiny and nature. The Word saves all creaturedom because, having taken upon Himself flesh like ours, He has brought Himself in contact with the entire material universe and introduced into it a seed of regeneration. The mark of the Divine Image is once again set upon mankind and the world, and with this is introduced the ferment of incorruptibility and immortality. Since human nature is by nature consubstantial to the divine and destined to develop itself in a deiform way, the oriental Church sees the Redemption not so much as a reparation for sin as a self-reparation of humanity and the world in Christ. A new divine communication is made in Christ to all humanity and the cosmos, so that the flesh may be spiritualized and man's spirit may proceed to divinization and thus to incorruptibility and immortality.

The incarnation is the means by which the Eternal Father realizes the union of the divine and the human. But this is to push into the background the aspect of redemption. Steeped in a platonic tradition, the oriental is much less interested in explaining theological realities in terms of efficient causality than he is in terms of participation. To Plato a thing is real insofar as it participates in the divine world of ideas. Augustine's contribution to Platonism was to realize that these divine ideas are the eternal verities within God Himself. Hence the oriental is more interested in the order of formal causality and in things as a participating similitude, an expression of God, than in the efficient causality by which they are produced.

When the oriental applies this point of view to the reality of grace he sees it primarily as a more perfect image and impression of the divinity upon man. Remaining within the framework of orthodoxy and clearly distinguishing grace from nature, he is less concerned with the distinction between grace and nature than with their continuity in the sense in which grace fulfills nature. Nature appears as an imperfect similitude of God which finds full realization and perfection in the divine similitude of grace. At times, even in western philosophy, one finds this definition of created being according to its intrinsic relationship to God. But the western

Church never fully accepted the platonic point of view, preferring to discuss created reality in terms of limited existence rather than in terms of formal causality and participation. The world for the western philosopher is as much a self-consistent world of natures and causes as an epiphany of a divine world. Efficient causality, the coming into existence, organization according to essence and existence, is a common viewpoint in the West. The West has great respect for created realities as such, in their own proper individuality and for the order of secondary causality. Viewing creatures as principles of activity, it insists very strongly upon the proper efficacy which God has granted to them. Hence, when the western theologian comes to discuss grace he treats it from the viewpoint of a new *power* added to nature—*super*-added to nature. To him it is a principle of new activity radically distinct from the activity of nature, and therefore his emphasis will be on the distinction between nature and grace.

Whereas the Orient centers itself and its considerations upon an ontology of things, the western Church is concerned more with their activity and with analysis of their mode of operation, particularly, as we have said, the order of efficient causality. When the oriental Church speaks of deification it means that process by which man's basic similitude to God is realized or fulfilled, so that he becomes accidentally consubstantial with God. This fulfillment takes place through grace, which represents a development of man's being, fulfilling and completing his native similitude with God. Deification is then a communication on the part of God of the conditions of existence proper to God Himself, incorruptibility and immortality. Man's being is lifted up so that he shares more fully, in the order of formal causality, in the divine being, with his entire human nature transformed by this participation.

The western Church speaks of the beatific vision as beatitude and understands this as a clear intuitive vision of God as He is in Himself. The term of man's existence, his destiny, is viewed less as a fulfillment of his similitude with God than as an operation in terms of power. Grace and glory are seen as subjective principles of activity on man's part. Grace, as a radical principle of supernatural operations, is conceived as a sharing in the divine nature insofar as this nature is a principle of acts properly and exclusively divine. Glory is that principle which empowers man to produce a beatifying act of vision. Since the western Church does not speak of an incomprehensible supra-essence distinct from the energies of God it cannot conceive of any natural participation in the nature of God insofar as this nature is exclusively proper to God. Instead it looks on grace and glory as a sharing in that principle of divine operation by which God takes Himself as an object and, perceiving Himself as He is, rejoices in this sight.

Just as eastern and western theology differ in their approach to the final beatitude towards which man is in progress, the West emphasizing the ethical actions which culminate in the act of vision and the East the fulfillment of similitude through deification, so also do they differ, as we have already indicated, in their concept of man. The oriental Church has always had a more mystical and religious conception of man, stressing the notion of man as an epiphany of God, with the image of God inscribed in his very being. The western Church, on the other hand, conceives man rather from the point of view of his nature as a source of specific operation, intellection and volition, and stresses the active, moral elements in ascetical practice. In the western Church nature is considered a potency ordained towards an end. Speaking much of man's final end, beatitude, which he is to attain through virtuous ethical and religious actions, the western Church accents the essential movement of man towards this supreme good of his soul. The oriental Church, however, prefers to stress the realization of the consubstantiality of the soul with God thanks to a progressive illumination of man's being.

Although the two spiritualities are quite similar in practice there are different emphases in ascetical theory. Western asceticism is concerned with the notion of self-conquest, conquest of the world and of matter, whereas eastern asceticism puts emphasis on the spiritualization of the world, its re-ordering to the spiritual. In the Orient, with its platonic tendencies, body is subordinate to soul less as an instrument which the soul uses in its spirituality than as an obstacle which may turn the soul away from the divine world of ideas. The body must be spiritualized by the soul and drawn into the light into which the intellect is plunged. In the West the subordination of body to soul is conceived as a service for the perfection of the soul, since it is through the body that the soul exercises its highest life. The Orient has an asceticism which emphasizes rather the spiritualization of matter, viewing the entire cosmos as something which the soul must illuminate. The soul begins the regeneration of the entire world and prepares it for "the new earth and the new heaven." In the West the world is something which man must conquer and dominate lest it be an obstacle to his contemplation. Man utilizes the world for his moral perfection.

The East regards Christ especially as the one who reconciles God and man on a cosmic plane and in the ontological order, whereas the West stresses the moral reconciliation of God with man; Christ undertakes to knit up our relationships with God. The function of Christ the Redeemer is visualized in the East as a restoration of the full nature of a being to its image-of-God quality. His work is seen as a re-creation, a regeneration, a re-spiritualization of human nature and of all things.

So, too, the East stresses the ontological and cosmic values of the incarnation and of the Eucharist. It is the Eucharist which continues here below the presence of Christ and His task of spiritualizing the cosmos. It is, as it were, the ferment of incorruptibility and the promise of a new world inserted into our human context until the *parousia* comes. The West, however, is more concerned with the moral actions of man and, in particular, with the notion of the Church militant.

It is obvious that each of these conceptions of grace and its relation to man can be reconciled with the other to the enrichment of both.

NOTES

1. This chapter is largely a paraphrase of M.-J. Congar's article, "La déification dans la tradition spirituelle de l'Orient, d'après une étude récente," *Vie spirituelle* (1935), [91]-[107], which summarizes the article of M. Lot Borodine on the subject: "La doctrine de la 'déification' dans l'Eglise grecque jusqu'au XIᵉ siècle," *Revue de l'histoire des religions* (1932), pp. 5-44; (1932), pp. 525-74; (1933), pp. 8-55. In presenting Congar's viewpoint here we do not intend to endorse a real distinction between the supra-essence of God and the divine, uncreated energies, but only a mental distinction. It appears that the distinction can be so interpreted. Cf. C. Moeller "Théologie de la grâce et oecuménisme," *Irénikon* (1955), pp. 19-56, especially p. 25. See also J. Meyendorff, *Introduction à l'étude de Gregoire Palamas* (Paris, Seuil, 1959), pp. 306-311.

This distinction between the supra-essence of God and the divine, uncreated energies has been the subject of considerable controversy. Western theologians generally believe that it was introduced by Palamas; theologians of the Orthodox Church claim that it can be found, at least germinally, in the doctrine of the early church fathers. It has also been claimed, by some theologians of both schools, that the distinction contradicts the notion of the divine simplicity. See V. Lossky, *Essai sur la Théologie Mystique de l'Eglise d'Orient* (Paris, Aubier, 1944), pp. 74-86, and C. Lialine, "The Theological Teaching of Gregory Palamas on Divine Simplicity," *Eastern Churches Quarterly* (1946), pp. 266-287.

APPENDIX IV

GRACE AND PHILOSOPHY

WE HAVE SEEN that with the coming of grace a physical change takes place in man, for the created gift of grace permeates the depths of his soul. That grace affects not merely the faculties of intellect and will but the entire soul is not a matter of faith, nor is it a matter of faith that grace is really distinct from the habit of infused charity; but these are the doctrines of St. Thomas and are today the more common opinions. St. Thomas maintains that sanctifying grace is really distinct from the habit of charity and is only remotely ordained toward action, whereas charity is directly and immediately orientated to action. Charity is essentially dynamic and grace is its foundation.

In order to realize that the soul itself is affected by sanctifying grace, we must consider the final end of man. If that end is supernatural, the beatific vision of God, and if man is to obtain it through his own efforts, then there must be something within him which elevates man permanently to this higher order. Man must be supernaturalized in being. Otherwise his acts in the supernatural order would not be fully his own. Faculties have their roots in the soul; hence it seems entirely to be expected that the ultimate principle of activity, the soul itself, should be elevated to the supernatural order. For man's meritorious acts are not merely received acts but acts which he posits. They are truly his own and are not merely peripherally identified with him. When man posits supernatural acts of faith without being in the state of grace he is using a faculty which has been elevated—for there is still within him the supernatural infused virtue of faith—but he is not elevated in his substance since he does not possess grace. This is obviously not the normal state of affairs. If acts are to be elevated, it is normal that the faculty should be elevated. If the faculty is elevated, it is normal that the soul, which is the source from which the faculty flows, should itself be elevated. Both faculty and essence should be proportioned to the end which they are attempting to reach. Since this end is a supernatural one it is normal that man should be proportioned to it in the essence of his soul. Although the sinner can still make an act of faith, it is less fully and completely his own because it is threatened by his lack of sanctifying grace.

Exactly what kind of being is sanctifying grace? To begin with, since sanctifying grace is something supernatural, we can analyze it only analogically; nor will it fit perfectly into any of the Aristotelian categories designed for natural being. The next thing we note is that grace is an *accident,* not a substance nor a substantial part of a being. Man is already, with his body and soul, completely constituted a human being, substantially complete. Since grace is something *added* to man, a complete substance, it is called an accident. Grace is a unique accident, however, because it functions very much like a new nature. From it, as from a new soul, flow the new faculties of faith, hope and charity, which are like new ways of believing, trusting and loving. It is not an accident in the ordinary sense of the word because it does not perfect man within the line of perfections to which he is susceptible naturally. It does not humanize man further; it divinizes. It is a supernatural accident.

Grace is an absolute type of accident, an ontological reality in itself. As an accident it must inhere in another and is unable to exist by itself. But sanctifying grace is not merely a new ethical relationship to God. It is rather a positive entity infused into the soul whose presence brings a new relationship to God. Grace is always wholly relative to the Giver, wholly reflecting God, who has given it. A similitude to God, the image of God who has given it, in itself it is something absolute, the real, internal change of justification. We can describe grace as a quality because it qualifies man's soul, rendering it "such," different from what it was before, somewhat as redness renders hair different from what it was when it was white. It is a quality by which the soul is now rendered holy, beautiful.

All accidents, as Aristotle said, are either quality or quantity; but grace is obviously not an accident of quantity. What kind of a quality, then, is it? Grace can best be described as a habit because it is permanent, a new permanent principle of being and life. Possessing it, man is different in the order of being and of action. Now, habits are either operative or entitative. An operative habit is one which is immediately ordained towards action. Grace, however, is only remotely ordained to action, is only a remote principle of man's supernatural activity even as the soul is a remote principle of his natural activity. We call grace, then, an entitative habit, because it affects the existence of the soul itself, not simply determining it to a particular mode of activity and making a particular activity more easy to it. We must be careful, however, not to conceive grace as something purely static. Although not immediately ordained to action, grace is the ultimate root of action. It is in the last analysis a dynamism or an élan proportioning man to the beatific vision and drawing him towards it. As St. Thomas insists, it is an inclination, an ordination to the beatific vision. It has therefore within it a dynamism, a principle of divine life. But no principle of divine life is given except to move to action, to orientate to divine things. It is possible to unite these two aspects, dynamism and the more static state, if one remembers that grace is inclined towards act not immediately but mediately. For grace connaturalizes man to make him a citizen of heaven, directing him towards God as his term, magnetizing him towards his ultimate supernatural end.

Grace is, moreover, an accident really distinct from the soul, for it comes to the soul after the soul has been in existence, giving it a manner of being, and it is separable from the soul. Grace should not be conceived as *some thing* but as a *way in which* some thing is. The soul is "thus" when it has grace, the soul acts "thus" when it has grace. Theologians usually say that because it is an accident grace is not created; it is the soul that is created graced. Grace is not something made separately and then passed on to man, but grace is what constitutes the man newly altered. Unless we underscore the ontological reality of grace we will never realize the radical transformation that God effects in man's life. On the other hand, unless we contemplate the moral aspects, we will never understand how grace sets up a dialogue between the soul and God by which He invites it to a life of intimacy with Him. Both realizations are necessary.

The Uncreated Good is also given and passes into the genuine possession of the soul in the state of grace. We miss much of what revelation teaches about grace if we are content with saying that a created gift, a new ontological accident, is put into the soul. For the Holy Spirit also is given to us, poured into us, diffused throughout our whole being.

Is this simply a way of saying that man is now on friendly terms with God, or does it mean something very real? And if to say that God inhabits the soul means something very real, what precisely does it mean? God is present everywhere, by His power everywhere sustaining things in being. He is everywhere by His essence, since all things imitate His essence. But since it is apparent from Sacred Scripture that He *inhabits* only the souls of the just, there is evidently a special way in which He dwells in and is possessed by the soul in grace. For the just man there are two kinds of sharing in the divine nature. He has what is called a formal sharing, the form of sanctifying grace. Because of this man has a similitude to God, for grace is supernatural. But he has also a terminative partnership with God, for the created gifts establish within man a new relationship with God by which God is said to inhabit his soul. Man then possesses the divine Trinity dwelling within him. Grace modifies man so he can possess God Himself. This new relationship is not grace, but grace is the cause of the new relationship.

In certain epochs of Catholic tradition, however, the inhabitation was scarcely spoken of, the whole emphasis, especially during the seventeenth century, being placed on the created gift of sanctifying grace. The important factor is really God's indwelling, but in order that God may indwell, there must be a change in the soul to prepare it, and this change is sanctifying grace. The Fathers speak more often of the divine indwelling. They do not say man is in the state of sanctifying grace; they say that he has the Holy Spirit. More recent theological thinking on sanctifying grace prefers the idea that it brings about the indwelling, thus reducing the status of the indwelling to that of an effect. But the indwelling is much more important than an effect, for it is God Himself who by His entrance gives us sanctifying grace and all other divine effects. The divine inhabitation is not simply one more effect of the created gift of grace. God Himself dwelling in the soul produces grace.

That God dwells in the just is a matter of Catholic faith. St. Paul repeats it continually, as do the Greek Fathers. That this Uncreated Gift of God is an ontological presence, a physical presence, distinct from the created gift of grace is a theologically certain doctrine— that is, the statement of a conclusion of a syllogism in which one premise is revealed by God, and the other is naturally certain.

It is also a deduction from revelation that grace is that which renders man capable of the inhabitation. The Council of Trent declares: "Unless we are reborn in Christ we shall never be justified."[1] The council supposes a rebirth to justification, but a rebirth implies some kind of sharing in the nature of the one from whom we are reborn. He who generates, communicates his nature. In the condemnation of Baius,[2] when the Church speaks of the sublimation and the exaltation of our nature, it uses the term *consortium*. Again in the Mass, at the pouring of the drop of water into the wine, we find: "Grant us to become sharers in His divinity as He became a sharer in our humanity." In the Preface of the Ascension we pray "that He may grant us to be sharers in His divinity," and in the Secret of the Fourth Sunday after Easter we read: "You have been made sharers in the one Highest Divinity." The schema of the Vatican Council too said that sanctifying grace gives us a special resemblance, a special likeness, to God and some kind of sharing in His nature. In the Council of Florence[3] we are told that in confirmation the Holy Spirit is conferred upon the just, and in Trent[4] man is said to be anointed with the Holy Spirit. In Leo XIII's encyclical *Divinum Illud* he speaks of the inhabitation and the operation of the Holy Spirit and the veneration that is due to the Holy Spirit dwelling in man. He states that the Holy Spirit does not only convey gifts to man (in sanctification) but that he gives Himself, that He is the supreme gift who proceeds from the mutual love of the Father and the Son and that He is said to be possessed by man as the gift of the Most High God. Moreover, Leo XIII goes on to explain that the Holy Spirit does not dwell in man merely in the way He dwells in all things, by His power, presence and essence; "He is in man not only as He is in things, but in order that He may be known and loved by man. Moreover, God dwells in the soul in grace, as in a temple in an entirely singular and intimate manner." Again: "This marvellous conjunction of man and God which is called the inhabitation differs only by condition or state from the state of the beatific vision."

In the liturgy also the Holy Spirit appears as the guest of the soul, and the gift of the Most High God. The idea of a gift obviously carries with it the transference of something from someone to another through love. If the Holy Ghost is a gift of the Most High God, it is into man's possession that He is given. In the Mass for Wednesday after Pentecost the priest prays: "May the Holy Spirit by His inhabitation, prepare us to become the worthy temples of His glory." On the Saturday after Pentecost, in the Introit of the Mass, we read: "The charity of God is poured forth in our hearts through the inhabiting Spirit, who is in us," and in the oration, "Into our minds and souls, God, we implore Thee, graciously pour the Holy Spirit."

Man is generated, born from God. Reborn in the waters of baptism, in the laver of regeneration, he has communicated to him a share in the nature of the generator. (John 1:12; 1 John 2:2-9; 1 John 1:3-9; 1 John 4:7; James 1:18.) This is the central idea of all Johannine epistles, life communicated to man from God.

The text of 2 Peter 1:4 calls Christians "sharers in the divine nature." This would be a clear proof of the divine *consortium* were it not for the possibility that the text may refer to heaven. In an earlier place we mentioned that in New Testament theology the last gifts are given now, at baptism. They are eschatological gifts but conferred now. In this most energetic expression of all in Scripture concerning the *consortium divinae naturae*, there is a double problem. Is Peter referring to the *consortium* which the Christian enjoys now? This would seem to be the case since he is speaking about gifts already received, as a result of which man should live an active spiritual life. It would follow, then, that Peter is not referring to the gifts of glory. If this is so, our insistence upon the continuity of grace and glory provides a solution: supposing him to have a participation of the divine life in heaven and the possession of grace here, then man clearly has a participation in the divine life here while on this earth. We cannot, however, be certain from this text that it is referring to a physical participation. The participation could be moral—a new way of thinking and not a new mode of being.

If, however, we take the writings of Peter and Paul together with the doctrine of St. John, we have a clearer scriptural position. Functioning as sons, we lack the inheritance of sons until we pass through the condition of death. Man has only the first fruits of the inheritance, grace. Peter's text by itself could also be interpreted to mean a sharing in the incorruptibility of God, rather than in His nature, for he might be speaking merely of immortality. The Greek and Roman Fathers frequently spoke of grace as a share in the incorruptibility of God because they were deeply impressed by the divine incorruptibility. To the pagan and Judaic mentality up to the last periods of Judaism, the notion of life after death was extremely vague. The Fathers, however, had a strong realization that God's life was eternal. Therefore, for them to say that man would share in eternal life was simply another way of saying that man has a share in the divine life.

In the early years of the Christian era particularly, a tremendous sadness darkened the whole cast of Roman thought, precisely because of the vagueness concerning an after-life. A note of sadness is heard through all Epicurean thought; for the pagan world did not know what the future held. From Christianity and the mystery religions of the East came the idea that man is immortal. Although the precise nature of this immortality is rather vague in many of the mystery religions, to the Fathers the primary element became the incorruptibility of God; to many of them it became the essential notion of God. He is unchangeable, eternal, indefectible happiness, and this implies the plenitude of life and existence. St. Thomas would have stated that God is Pure Act and argued from that fact that there is no shadow of change or corruption possible to Him. The early Fathers, however, approached the question from the opposite direction. What impressed them was the plenitude of life, of incorruptible, eternal life in the Father, and the plenitude of holiness and goodness which God enjoys. Man, they say, shares in this. This may have been what Peter meant, that man shares in a divine characteristic, the divine immortality. Sharing in the divine immortality he shares, logically, also in the divine nature.[5]

That the Holy Spirit dwells within the Christian is clear from Romans 5:5; Romans 8:9, 1 Cor. 2:12, Galatians 4:6. Paul constantly asserts that the Spirit is poured into us, is given to us, dwells within us, that we are members of Christ, that we have His Spirit, the Spirit of Christ, the Spirit of the Father. The difficulty is to determine whether St. Paul is speaking of the Holy Spirit, or the created gift of grace. Certain texts lighten the darkness however. Paul tells us that the Holy Spirit seals the soul, dwells within the soul, remains in the soul, is in us, is received by us, is given to us, comes to us, is sent to us. St. John's account of Christ's words at the last supper, promising that if the Christian keeps His commandments the Father and He will come to him and take up Their abode with him make clear that the Father and Son will come to the just. Christ is not speaking merely to the apostles, for in verse 23 of chapter 14 He refers to all those who keep His commandments. Obviously Christ is speaking here of the three Persons of the Trinity, and not just of a created gift. The notion that man possesses the Holy Spirit is to be found also in Romans 8:9, "the spirit of God dwells in you," and in Ephesians 1:14, "you . . . were sealed with the Holy Spirit."

An indirect proof of our thesis comes from the Fathers' demonstration of the divinity of the Holy Spirit. Man, they argued, is divinized. Yet only God can divinize. Therefore the Holy Spirit, who divinizes man, is God. Obviously this proof has no force unless one assumes that the Holy Spirit divinizes man by His presence. The very being of the Godhead is somehow handed over to man, to be in his possession.

God then lives in the just in a way different from that in which He lives in others. The foundation of this presence, sanctifying grace, is in the real, ontological order. Thus between the divinity and the soul possessing sanctifying grace there is an accidental union, and the *bond* itself, grace, is that which, in a marvellous way, unites the substance of man to the substance of God in an accidental fashion.

NOTES

1. Denzinger 795.
2. Denzinger 1021.
3. Denzinger 697.
4. Denzinger 799.
5. De Bovis, *op. cit.,* p. 85.